THE MIND OF SANTAYANA

THE MIND OF SANTAYANA

RICHARD BUTLER, O.P.

GREENWOOD PRESS, PUBLISHERS
NEW YORK   1968

Dedicated in Memoria
To Two Wise Philosophers,
My Mother and Father

Author's Preface

ON SEPTEMBER 26th, 1952, in his 89th year, George Santayana died in Rome.

Shortly afterwards I wrote my "Memories of Santayana" for *Commonweal* magazine (Oct. 24, Oct. 31, 1952). The response was overwhelming. I am still receiving letters from interested readers, some of them inquiries about the publication of this critical study of Santayana's philosophy. In my articles I had mentioned this professional basis of my personal association with him.

At the bid of my superiors, I went to Rome in the Fall of 1950 to work for my doctorate in philosophy at the Angelicum. A dissertation, an original contribution to my field of study, was a requirement for the degree. Having no preferred subject, I consulted the dean of the department. He suggested that I do a critical analysis of George Santayana's philosophy, pointing out that Santayana's influence had been strong in the development of American trends in philosophy; and that he was residing in Rome and might provide personal consultation during the progress of the work.

The possibility of working with living thought, actually consulting the subject of my study, was appealing. But was it possible? Would Santayana cooperate in a criticism of his philosophy: the fruit of a long lifetime of professional labor weighed and valued by a young graduate student?

He did, and he was very gracious about it. In fact, he welcomed an intrinsic criticism of his philosophy. "Show me, if you can," he said, "where I go off the track of straight speculation."

I dare to think, however, that he welcomed much more my weekly visits which extended over two years, right up to a few months before his death. He was fixed in his philosophy, a completed and closed system, but he was accessible as a friend. A former teacher, he was at home with young students, especially those who had enjoyed a classical and liberal education. He favored my faith, although he did not share it, and he explicitly admired my vocation. Even the religious Order of my profession was familiar and attractive to him. In his youthful period of wishful religious thinking he had once expressed a desire to be a Dominican preacher and scholar. Furthermore, the Dominican friars of his native Avila had attended his beloved sisters in their last illnesses. We also shared a love for Boston and its environs, where he and I had spent our youth—many years apart. In spite of our differences, in age, background, and convictions, we had enough in common to make a sincere and lasting friendship.

In the "Memories" I mentioned the triad relationship between us. Philosophically, I was his critic. He represented a curious combination of Platonic idealism, Kantian transcendentalism, and the crude materialism of Democritus. My own philosophical training and conviction was moderately realistic, in the hylomorphic tradition of Aristotle and Aquinas. Religiously, I was his spiritual father, anxious to help a lost child find his way home. Personally, I was his friend. I was pleased when readers of the "Memories" noted and mentioned a strain of personal affection in those reflections. This exclusively critical study is, by nature and intent, an objective analysis and evaluation, disallowing any subjective dispositions. For that reason I take this opportunity to comment briefly on my personal association with the man whose philosophy I am criticizing.

I value highly my friendship with George Santayana during the last months of his life. Already I frequently find myself reminiscing with delight as I recall the familiar walk up to *Monte Celio:* along the *Via dei Fori Imperiali,* where the skeletal forums of the Caesars are still silhouetted against the Mediterranean blue of the Italian sky; around the south rim of the Colosseum, a gigantic, grim shell of an arena once sodden with the blood of beasts and gladiators and martyrs; up the *Via Claudia,* bordered by the jutting substructures of Agrippina's temple; then on to the *Via San Stefano Rotondo,* named for the fifth century circular church on the corner. Adjacent to the church is a jagged stretch of the original city wall, broken by the sudden entrance into the paved driveway of trim, modern Calvary Hospital, administered by the Sisters of the Little Company of Mary. Here in seclusion, in retirement and ill health, Santayana spent the last twelve years of his life.

There is much remembered of those weekly visits: the glad greeting, always by handshake according to European custom; the tea and imported English cookies; the literary experience shared, something read or written; the long conversations: about poetry and philosophy, history and art, persons and places recalled. (Religion was a subject out of bounds, by his manifest intent. It was too late, even for consideration. He had committed his choice to paper, to many pages of many books.) We would talk through the dusk, into darkness, for the light hurt his eyes. Then good-by again—until that final farewell when he stood leaning against the door saying: "I won't see you again. Now I am alone."

The personal association is over and it is time for a critical appraisal, not of the man, but of his philosophy.

For two years I studied his writings, approximately thirty volumes and as many pertinent articles. I had the advantage of using his own copies, with their valuable marginal annotations. And I checked any difficult or obscure passage for exact interpretation either with Santayana himself, or with Daniel Cory, his former secretary and, by Santayana's description, the best exponent of his philosophy. Over two years more have passed, in which I have continued my research and have gained, I think, the advantage of mature reflection.

The only work of Santayana's I have not cited, except for one passage, is the *Life of Reason*. Although this work, which originally appeared in five volumes in 1905-1906, has been considered by many critics to be his greatest contribution to philosophy, Santayana deprecated the whole work as immature and asked me not to use it, insisting that there was hardly a word in it he would not change after mature reflection. Scribners has brought out posthumously a revised edition, abridged into one volume. But Santayana told me that he had no enthusiasm, and too little energy, to do much work on this revision during the last year of his life. The task fell to Cory, for the most part, and was completed by constant cross-reference to Santayana's mature synthesis. This mature synthesis of Santayana's philosophy is contained in *Scepticism and Animal Faith* and the four books collectively titled *Realms of Being*. Following Santayana's direction, I have concentrated on these works, without, however, neglecting the others.

The time has come for such a critical appraisal of Santayana's thought. His last word has been written and published; his philosophical doctrine, mature and considered, is complete; his influence is determined. Much more time must pass before any judgment can be made about the penetration and permanence of that influence. Even now, however,

I do not hesitate to predict a much more effective and lasting literary influence than a purely philosophical one.

Santayana taught philosophy at Harvard University for 23 years, and held its chair of philosophy during the last five of those years. He was prominent among the Neo-Realists (a strange label for Santayana) who grappled with the epistemological problem during the early part of this century. He has written prodigiously and his books have enjoyed extensive circulation in England and America.

The course of modern philosophy is fickle, unpredictable, and the trends are ever changing their directions. Yet it is safe to say that Santayana may well be the last essentialist. The existentialists are having their day; and, in spite of their extravagances and short-sightedness, they are groping at least in the direction of a sound realism which has always merited a more universal respect and a more lasting recognition. Essentialism is a speculative luxury for romanticists which our desperate contemporary society—with its high cost of living at all—cannot afford.

As for the popular reception of his books, I am convinced that this is an indication of deserved literary appreciation. I have met many people who have read Santayana, and extensively, but not one of them evinced a clear understanding of his philosophical doctrine. They are fascinated, understandably, by his cultured charm, his keen insights, and exquisite literary craftsmanship. But they appreciate his words more than his meaning.

Perhaps, then, this book can be of service as an exposition of the philosophical structure supporting his artistry. But I hope that this critical study will be a service of greater value by proving the intrinsic weakness of any philosophical structure that is composed of an impossible scepticism, an unnatural transcendentalism, and an irrational presupposition of materialism.

My gratitude must be expressed: to my superiors, who gave me the opportunity to do this work; to Fr. Evaristus Moran, O.P., Dean of the Department of Philosophy at the Angelicum, who suggested it; to Fr. Ambrose McNicholl, O.P., Professor of Modern Philosophy in the same department, who directed and guided it. I am also indebted to many people, too many to name, who encouraged me and assisted me in preparing the manuscript for publication. Particularly, however, I want to thank Mr. Chauncey Stillman of New York City, who has prodded me every step of the way and has provided me with valuable materials. The six original manuscripts of Santayana's major works, donated by Mr. Stillman, are now in the library of St. Rose Priory in Dubuque, Ia.

RICHARD BUTLER, O.P., *Chaplain*
Aquinas Hall Newman Center
University of New Mexico
Albuquerque, N. Mex.

Contents

Part I—Background

But what we think probable hangs on our standard of probability and of evidence; the spiritual experiences that come to us are according to our disposition and affections; and any new philosophy we frame will be an answer to the particular problems that beset us, and an expression of the solutions we hope for.

GEORGE SANTAYANA
Winds of Doctrine

Introductory Note

On Temperament in Modern Philosophy

Of whatever temperament a professional philosopher is, he tries when philosophizing, to sink the fact of his temperament. Temperament is no conventionally recognized reason, so he urges impersonal reasons only for his conclusions. Yet his temperament really gives him a stronger bias than any of his more strictly objective premises.—WILLIAM JAMES [1]

WHEN William James introduced his version of pragmatic philosophy to a Boston audience in the first decade of this century, he prefaced his presentation with some remarks on the temperamental character of modern philosophy. James traced two types of temperament manifested in the more recent course of philosophical speculation. With characteristic boldness of expression, he pointed out that the "tender-minded" are drawn towards rationalism, while the "tough-minded" are attracted to empiricism.

James recognized the strong influence of subjective disposition on the modern philosopher's interpretation of nature: its structure and composition, inter-relations, values, and teleological significance, if any. C. E. M. Joad has made a similar observation: "To some extent we all construct the universe in our own image, and fashion the world after our heart's desire. Thus while philosophy gives us much information about the universe, it gives us much, perhaps more,

· 3 ·

about the philosopher. It is a description of the cosmos; but it is also a personal confession." [2]

These personal, even confessional, elements in philosophy are neither essential nor traditional to the science. They do characterize what James calls the "professional philosopher" —often a suffering introspective who elaborates his own opinions and then trades them in the marketplace or displays them in the salons of dilettantes. Subjectivism—holding a mirror up to man, a particular man, rather than to nature —has haunted modern philosophy since Descartes began to spin his web of meditations.

The ancients, even the primitive Ionic cosmologists, exercised a healthy intellectual objectivity. They looked out into the universe, not into themselves, when they sought the ultimate causes of reality. Except for the few sceptical sophists, who appear in every age, the Greek philosophers did not question the efficacy of their cognitive powers. They did not doubt their ability to reach into reality. They studied things, all things, and not merely the data of their own consciousness. Only individual intellectual acumen exerted a personal influence on the conclusions they reached.

From internal evidence, by examining their writings, we can discover very little personal information about the early philosophers. Thanks to his literary form of dramatic dialogue, Plato has supplied us with considerable information about the person of Socrates. But from these same dialogues we learn hardly anything about their author, other than to recognize a reflected loftiness of thought and intent. The detached scientific procedure of Aristotle denies us any access to the temperament or personality of the Stagirite.

The medieval philosophers continued this same tradition of impersonal speculation. Error, for them, was a matter of a syllogistic misstep, not an expression of personal maladjustment. The Scholastics, at least in their ascendancy, used their logical instruments as proper tools of research into reality. The keen synthetic mind of St. Thomas Aquinas, reaching beyond the grasp of Aristotle, realized the natural structure of reality in its ultimate principles. But it was a synthesis that he discovered, not a system that he imposed. As a contemporary Thomist points out: "Thomism is not a system because it is not a philosophy of ideas but a philosophy of being; it does not enclose being in a formula but rather seeks that which is formal and actual in being (*esse*)." [3]

From the voluminous works of Aquinas, the hagiographer will uncover precious little information about his subject beyond the evidence of a sublime intellect clearly penetrating existence. The saint retires behind his syllogisms, emerging only to salute his Creator when he pushes his arguments into His presence. If an inquirer sought indications of temperament from Thomas' philosophical treatises alone, he easily might conclude a cold and calculating temper, devoid of feeling or fancy. Could this same rigid scientist be the ecstatic saint, the Poet of the Eucharist, who composed such fiery expressions of love and adoration in his Mass for Corpus Christi? Only in an age when philosophy was recognized as objective wisdom, not an accommodation of subjective disposition.

The decline of Scholastic speculation and the rise of empiric investigation stirred the mathematical mind of René Descartes to usher in a new direction of philosophy, one which has elevated the philosopher above philosophy. Considering himself inspired to reconstruct the natural synthesis, not from nature's bosom but from his own, Descartes established the sceptical method of universal doubt. Thence began that interminable retreat from reality that has characterized philosophical speculation ever since.

No longer are we invited to observe and probe the universe before our eyes. Instead we must close our eyes, reach into the recesses of our own mind (or somebody else's), and from its cleansed laboratories excogitate a reconstruction of the universe. This reconstruction inevitably is stamped with the particular type of mind that makes it. Descartes was a mathematician, and to his rebuilding of the philosophical edifice he brought his mathematical method, with all its deductive demands of precision and clarity and measured calculation. He began to build his monumental geometric design that would rise from the simple to the complex and embrace the whole of reality. He set about his ambitious task seeking assurance of certitude:

> And I had little difficulty in determining the objects with which it was necessary to commence, for I was already persuaded that it must be with the simplest and easiest to know, and considering that of all those who have hitherto sought truth in the sciences, the mathematicians alone have been able to find any demonstrations, that is, any certain and evident reasons, I did not doubt that such must have been the rule of their investigations.[4]

Certainty, then, would rest on the clear idea rather than the evident object. Thus ended that healthy philosophical climate in which one reasoned from external evidence. Instead the mind turns in upon itself, and in place of demonstration we have meditation. As Thomas P. Neill has pointed out: "Descartes does not reason with his reader, as at least the better philosophers had done in days gone by. He does not proceed, as ordinary men do, reasoning his way, step by step. He dogmatizes instead. He reasons, it is true, but not with the reader. He meditates; he reasons with himself. The reader must follow, and the implication always lurks in his pages that if you do not follow, if you disagree, there is something wrong with your mind. Descartes is always dogmatically right."[5]

Thus, too, egotism became the fulcrum of philosophy; and the followers of Descartes, discarding traditional terminology and method and all the findings of their predecessors, set out afresh, each to make his own reconstruction of reality. Perhaps that egotism is nowhere more pronounced than in Descartes' own reconstruction, evident in his very first postulate. As Paul Valery observes: "The *Cogito* sounds for him a clarion to his essential egotism. He comes back to it again and again as the theme of his lucid *Me,* a reveille blown to pride and to the well-springs of his being. Never before him had any philosopher so deliberately displayed himself upon the stage of his own thought, showing himself off, daring to use the first personal pronoun throughout whole pages. . . ." [6]

Descartes distorted man, dividing body from soul and establishing a dichotomy between mind and matter, thought and extension: a dualism that has affected nearly every philosopher after him. As Gilson correctly concludes: "Metaphysics then is pure spiritualism, and physics pure mechanism." And subsequent philosophy tended towards either extreme as a whole solution to the problems it raised, depending, in large measure, on the philosopher's particular temperament.

Descartes' exclusively introspective approach to problems of philosophy turned the philosopher's attention from *what is* to *what is my opinion.* An inquirer no longer asks what is the philosophy of nature, but, indicating a particular person, asks what is *his* philosophy. In most universities the teaching of philosophy has become an eclectic exposition of the history of particular men and their opinions. The *Cogito* of Descartes ripped philosophy away from its moorings in reality and set it adrift in the hazardous flux of individual conscious experience.

Immanuel Kant tried to steer philosophical speculation

through certain categories. These were not, however, the categories of being discovered by Aristotle. They were categories of the mind imposed by Kant. By his transcendental criticism of knowledge, Kant cut the subjective mind away from objective reality, completing the devastating cleavage begun by Descartes. He proudly asserted he had succeeded in supplying solutions to all the problems of metaphysics, which, in effect, he had destroyed.[7] Kant struck the decisive blow, splitting nature so that her future students would see only half her figure. The "tender-minded" saw her as a romantic internal idea; the "tough-minded" noted only her rough external appearance. Rational idealism and empiric phenomenalism claimed her embrace and fought each other for her favor.

Subsequent philosophers, however, were not united in their respective camps. Subjective philosophy is individualistic, making as many philosophies as philosophers. It would not be difficult, nor arbitrary nor haphazard, to pick out a dominant personal theme in nearly all modern systems of philosophy. A distinctive motif appears in each subjective system, expressing in some way the personality of its author. This is an inevitable result of too much introspection and too little observation. Transcendentalism is the first and fatal step away from objectivity. The man on the street does not doubt his immediate contact with the ambient world, but the philosopher in his study unhesitatingly follows Kant in transcending real existence to explore the content of his own consciousness. What emerges, if anything can, is a product of the environment in which it was born.

The importance of temperament, of all personal dispositions, cannot be overlooked in the examination of the philosophy of a contemporary. William James, in his blunt style, strongly emphasizes the effect of temperament on a philosopher:

It loads the evidence for him one way or the other, making for a more sentimental or a more hard-hearted view of the universe, just as this fact or that principle would. He *trusts* his temperament. Wanting a universe that suits it, he believes in any representation of the universe that does suit it. He feels men of opposite temper to be out of key with the world's character, and in his heart considers them incompetent and "not in it," in the philosophic business, even though they may far excel him in dialectical ability. Yet in the forum he can make no claim, on the bare ground of his temperament, to superior discernment or authority. There arises thus a certain insincerity in our philosophic discussion; the potentest of all our premises is never mentioned.[8]

These introductory remarks on temperament in modern philosophy are not made in anticipation of dwelling exclusively, or inordinately, upon the personal elements in Santayana's philosophy. But what James calls "the potentest of all our premises" should be considered adequately and properly.

George Santayana elaborated an introspective philosophy. Personal and temperamental influences have left their marks upon it, especially in his concentration on the intuition of essence. Santayana warned his readers that "any new philosophy we frame will be an answer to the particular problems that beset us, and an expression of the solutions we hope for."[9] In that spirit he framed a philosophy remarkably attuned to his own temperament and obviously contrived to provide a solution to the particular problems that beset him.

I have, therefore, extended the customary biographical sketch, recognizing his personal background as a kind of remote cause of the direction of his philosophy. His philosophical background appears in the position of a proximate cause; and a brief account of the Critical Neo-Realism movement describes the particular occasion which brought into prominence the notion of essence: the keystone of Santayana's philosophy. In describing his personal background, I have stressed two aspects of his life: religious conflict and the desire for solitude. Such an emphasis is justified by the evidence of his public meditations.

Chapter One

Personal Background

HOW came a child born in Spain of Spanish parents to be educated in Boston and to write in the English language?"[1] This introductory line of an autobiographical sketch indicates the conflicting influences in the personal background of George Santayana.

He was born in Madrid on the 16th of December, 1863, and baptized there in the Catholic Church of San Marcos sixteen days later. Soon afterwards his family moved to Avila. Here in that ancient walled city in the hills of Castile the future philosopher passed his early childhood. When he was nine years old, however, he was uprooted from his Spanish soil and transplanted to America. From a tranquil and traditional heritage he suddenly encountered the New World, still boisterous and bustling in the growing pains of its youth. The cause of this violent change, which was to influence the philosopher's life so strongly, was a family affair.

His mother, Josefina Borrás, was a child of parents engaged in colonial service. Her father was, for a time, a political exile: first in Glasgow, where Josefina was born, then in Virginia. Later, by the appointment of Andrew Jackson, he returned to Spain as American Consul in Barcelona. After ten years in that position his appointment terminated, but a change of political fortune enabled him to obtain another post in Manila under Spanish auspices. His wife did not make this last trip with him, but he insisted on taking his daughter.

During the six-month voyage to the Philippines, Santayana presumes, his mother was indoctrinated by his grandfather, "a Deist, and ardent disciple of Rousseau, and, I suspect, a Freemason." [2] At least, he tells us, she often quoted the commonplace maxims of "the Enlightenment," especially those culled from Pope's *Essay on Man*, and considered "all else [to be] unnecessary in religion or morality." [3] She had been baptized a Catholic, motivated by social necessity during her years in Barcelona, but apparently never practiced her faith. Speaking of her delayed baptism, and first confession and communion, Santayana says:

> This wealth of sacraments, raining down on her unprepared and extraordinary self-reliant little soul, seems not to have left much hunger for further means of grace. My mother always spoke of such things as of troublesome and empty social requirements. . . .[4]

When he arrived in the Philippines, Santayana's grandfather was reassigned to the governorship of one of the smaller islands. After his death a few years later, his daughter, Josefina, lived with friends in Manila. Here she met and married George Sturgis, a proper and Protestant Bostonian. Five children were born of this union; two of them died in infancy. Sturgis died young and his widow, mindful of an earlier promise to raise the children in America, returned to her husband's family in Boston. After three years in this alien atmosphere, she took her three children back to Spain with her.

In Madrid, five years later, the widow married a second time. Her new husband, Don Augustín Ruiz de Santayana, had succeeded to the post vacated by her father's death; but a few years later he had returned to Spain. There was one child born of this marriage: Jorge, later to assume the briefer and anglicized form of his name—George Santayana.

The boy developed a strong attachment to his father and to his father's way of thinking. As a young child, and in later years when he returned to Avila for occasional visits, he often accompanied his father on long walks, absorbing the older man's attitude on various subjects: an admiration for English efficiency, a distrust of speculation in favor of immediate fact, a liking for the poetry of Lucretius, especially in its condemnation of religion as a sham born of fear and wonder and foisted upon the ignorant.

A curious separation occurred when Santayana was six years old. His mother decided to fulfill the promise made to her first husband; she took the three Sturgis children with her and went back to Boston. George stayed in Avila with his father for the next three years. This unsatisfactory arrangement was dissolved in 1872 when the father brought George to Boston. The family was reunited only briefly, however, for the father soon returned to stay in Avila.

Thus began an entirely new life in America for nine year-old George Santayana. Undoubtedly those early years of adjustment were difficult ones. A new language, new customs and religion that were not at all in harmony with the old ways, a new set of relatives, staid and stolid. In this alien environment the seeds of solitude developed in the sensitive foreign boy, much more mature than his classmates. He attended Miss Welchman's Kindergarten on Chestnut Street, then the Brimmer public school, finally the historic Boston Latin School. In later reflections he admits this early feeling of estrangement from the more familiar and more favored:

> For by chance I was a foreigner where I was educated; and although the new language and customs interested me and gave me no serious trouble, yet speculatively and emotionally, especially in regard to religion, the world around me was utterly undigestible. . . .

And as the feeling of being a stranger and an exile, by nature as well as by accident, grew upon me in time, it came to be almost a point of pride; some people may have thought it an affectation. It was not that. I have always admired the normal child of his age and country. My case was humanly unfortunate and involved many defects; yet it opened to me another vocation, not better (I admit no absolute standards) but more speculative, freer, juster, and for me happier.[5]

The family lived in a modest home on Beacon Street, within the shadow of the state capitol. Later they moved to Roxbury, a nearby suburb. From the beginning there was religious conflict. The influential Sturgis relatives wanted the newcomers to participate in Unitarian worship, so completely contrasted to their traditional Catholic atmosphere. Susana, George's older sister, was a practicing Catholic throughout her life. She taught her young half-brother his catechism and hustled him off to early Mass on Sundays, before the boy was taken to Unitarian services. His own sense of belonging was Catholic, while the pared and grim services at King's Chapel evoked a repugnance he never overcame. He later described the Unitarian chapel as a place where:

> . . . good people in their Sunday clothes, so demure, so conscious of one another, not needing in the least to pray or to be prayed for . . . [came] to hear a sermon like the leading article in some superior newspaper, calculated to confirm the conviction already in them that their bourgeois virtues were quite sufficient and that perhaps in time poor backward races and nations might be led to acquire them.[6]

Even towards the end of his life, in his last book, he spoke of the free Protestant churches as supplying "a nook for quietness and a Sabbath refuge, feeble in thought, null in organization, animated by little more than traditional or censorious sentiment to be applied to current opinion and to the conduct of lay life."[7]

That these early conflicts, arising from religious and environmental difficulties, set him on the course of detachment and solitude, he clearly indicates in his memoirs. Speaking of those childhood years in Back Bay Boston, he says:

> I was unhappy there. At school nothing was imposed on me that I could complain of; there were no grinding tasks and no punishments; but until the last two or three years, when I formed close friendships and awoke to literature, it was all dead routine, and insufficient. A great void remained, which nothing at home could fill. The family was deeply disunited, and each member unhappy for a different reason.[8]

There is a natural adjustment demanded in adolescence to bridge the gulf between childhood and manhood. Santayana had to cope with these additional difficulties which affected his development, engendering attitudes that later on would influence the whole pattern of his philosophy. This is his own interpretation:

> I know my feelings in those years were intense, that I was solitary and unhappy, out of humor with everything that surrounded me, and attached only to a persistent dream-life, fed on books of fiction, on architecture, and on religion. I was not precocious; I may have had more ability than the average boy, but it was lavished on boyish thoughts; and a certain backwardness, or unwilling acceptance of reality, characterizes my whole life and philosophy, not indeed as a maxim but as a sentiment.[9]

Santayana was a good student from his earliest years. He preferred study in solitude, a few close friends with mutual interests, a retreat from the burdensome reality of crowded and noisy social life. According to a classmate of his high school years, the young Spaniard was often subject to the taunts of other boys, "but a sharp tongue and a fiery temper made him well able to take care of himself." [10]

At sixteen he wrote his first, and a prize-winning, poem, "full of pessimistic, languid, Byronic sentiments, describing

the various kinds of superiority that Night has over Day." [11]
He joined a debating society, was favored for a position in
the Boston School Regiment, and by his senior year of high
school he enjoyed some prestige among his schoolmates, especially in their recognition of his literary talents. On grad-
uating from Boston Latin School, he took entrance examina-
tions for Harvard, successfully and with the distinction of
six honorable mentions.

Throughout his high school years he had clung to his affection for things Catholic. He often attended the collegiate
church attached to Boston College. Here he listened to sermons by successive presidents of the college, Father Fulton
and Father O'Connor. "Catholic preachers," he remarked,
"at least are expected to preach the Gospel, and not some
message new to the age." [12] He admired their dialectic and
their sentiment, and always remained cognizant of the internal logic of Catholic doctrine. He loved the sensibles and
ceremonies in the Church, but never approached the sacra-
ments.

There was always a mixture of longing and sensible satisfaction clashing with a youthful pessimism bred of contact
with the harsh realities of life. At sixteen, he composed a
poem addressed *To the Host*, which, he said, was "clear in
faith's divine moonlight" and "my only friend;" but then he
sighed that his faith was "too much like despair." He admitted his deep desire for peace, but:

> For this purpose the machinery of the sacraments was not
> needed. I had no wish to go to confession and communion,
> else I should have done so. My faith was indeed so like de-
> spair that it wasn't faith at all; it was fondness, liking. What
> in Spanish is called *afición;* I indulged in it, but only north-
> north-west, and keeping my freedom. I heartily agreed with
> the Church about the world, yet I was ready to agree with
> the world about the Church; and I breathed more easily in
> the atmosphere of religion than in that of business, precisely

because religion, like poetry, was more ideal, more freely imaginary, and, in a material sense, falser.[13]

These pro and con religious thoughts increased during college years, stimulated by a new venture into the vagaries of modern philosophy. The vague scepticism and materialism he had acquired from his father took definite form, were even expressed in impressive scientific terms, at Harvard University. Naturalism, the popular doctrine of the period, relegated the supernatural to the superstitions of the ignorant. At Harvard one was educated. The ultimate resolution of Santayana's internal conflict was inevitable.

Santayana's undergraduate years at Harvard satiated his habitual hunger for study and solitude. There were a few choice friends, membership in societies that his meager allowance could afford; but he preferred his simple room in the Yard, where he stayed during the school-week, and a particular tiny alcove in the University library where he digested a daily fare of philosophical books and literary periodicals. On weekends he would take the horse-car to his mother's home in Roxbury, his handy copy of Lucretius' *De Rerum Natura* in his pocket. During these years, he says: "I recited my Lucretius with as much gusto as my St. Augustine; and gradually Lucretius sank deeper and became more satisfying." [14]

He contributed cartoons to the *Lampoon* and poems to *Harvard Monthly*. During these undergraduate years he found college life pleasant enough; and, through his studies, he gradually formulated a few of the principles that would govern his philosophy and his life. The summer following his freshman year he returned to Avila for a visit with his father. Now in some measure adjusted to the New World, he found himself a stranger in the Old. He was never to feel wholly at home in either.

His half-sister Susana, who had tried to share her faith with him, entered a Carmelite convent in Baltimore at this time. She was then in her middle thirties. After six months in the novitiate she left. Later she returned to Avila and married a widower; she remained a devout Catholic until the end of her life. Santayana's other half-sister, Josefina, also returned to Avila later on and was reconciled to the Church before her death. Commenting on Susana's faith and the loss of her religious vocation, the philosopher of the family boldly declared:

> I understood what she taught me very much better than she did, and I had a much greater affinity than she to a religious life. She tried it and couldn't bear it; I could have borne it gladly if I had wished to try it. . . .
>
> Now I was aware, at first instinctively and soon quite clearly on historical and psychological grounds, that religion and all philosophy of that kind was *invented*. It was all conceived and worked out inwardly, imaginatively, for moral reasons; I could have invented or helped to invent it myself, if I had gone in for it; and I could have accepted it and enlarged it by my own insights if, like all original souls, I had fancied myself inspired.[15]

By the time Santayana had completed his college studies, the religious conflict of his youth was resolved. The *afición* would always remain, but he no longer stood, as he once described it poetically, "at the church door," looking in and longing for what he refused to accept. Faith, he decided with his parents, was a fiction of the imagination; but, unlike them, he could see nothing bad in any creative work of the imagination as long as one did not take it for fact. He rejected not only the supernatural but, in so far as he could, the natural arena of worldly life. His choice was a retreat into solitude where he could cultivate his imagination and "fill it with endless forms." There he would discover the keystone of his mature philosophy.

No, said I to myself, even as a boy: they [the works of human imagination] are good, they alone are good; and the rest—the whole real world—is ashes in the mouth. My sympathies were entirely with those other members of my family who were devout believers. I loved the Christian epic, and all those doctrines and observances which bring it down into daily life: I thought how glorious it would have been to be a Dominican friar, preaching that epic eloquently, and solving afresh all the knottiest and sublimest mysteries of theology. . . . For my own part I was quite sure that life was not worth living; for if religion was false everything was worthless; and almost everything if religion was true. In this youthful pessimism I was hardly more foolish than so many amateur medievalists and religious esthetes of my generation. I saw the same alternative between Catholicism and complete disillusion: but I was never afraid of disillusion, and I have chosen it.[16]

At Harvard, Santayana studied under William James and Josiah Royce, then young professors boldly professing and teaching "the dangers and scandals of free thought, all the more disquieting in that their free thought enveloped religion."[17] Bowen and Palmer also were among his teachers, eclectically expounding random theories in the history of philosophy. Upon completing his college work, Santayana shared the Walker Fellowship for advanced philosophical study in Germany with a classmate, Charles Augustus Strong, who was to remain a close friend for half a century. He received his bachelor's degree *summa cum laude* and sailed for Europe: another visit to Avila, then to Dresden to learn German; finally to Berlin for his studies.

This was in 1886. At the University of Berlin he studied under Paulsen. But he found the German spirit of "uniforms, music and beer" alien to his own, and his philosophy courses at the University a disappointment. After one semester, Strong relinquished his part of the scholarship and left; Santayana, after spending a semester in England, returned to Berlin with even less enthusiasm. The intricacies of idealistic philosophy confused and annoyed him. His interest in philosophy was not as a science but, as he said, "only as a balance of mind and temper, in which all the sciences and arts should compose as true a picture as possible of nature and human nature." [18]

Discontented with his surroundings and his study, he asked permission to return to Harvard and use his fellowship allowance for resident graduate work there. This unusual request was granted and Santayana returned, completing his work at home, a critical dissertation on Lotze, and attending seminars conducted by James and Royce. Upon receiving his doctorate in philosophy in 1889, he was taken immediately into the Harvard faculty. He was an instructor for nine years, an associate professor for an additional nine years. When Royce died, Santayana succeeded his former professor and obtained the University's chair of philosophy, holding it until he left Harvard in 1912.

Doctor Santayana did not feel at home at Harvard, or, for that matter, in America. He was still the wandering stranger, looking forward to the summer vacation when he could travel abroad, preferably to England. Here he found some sentimental affinity in assuming the life of an English gentleman, with proper quarters on Jermyn Street in St. James. He was friendly with Earl Russell and Lionel Johnson. His friend of undergraduate days, Charles Strong, had married John D. Rockefeller's daughter. She became a mental patient and died soon afterwards. Strong, after unsuccessfully attempting teaching positions at Cornell and Columbia, retired and took up residence in Europe. Santayana often visited him in Paris, and later at his villa in Fiesole. He spent two complete years in Europe during his teaching tenure: one (1896-1897) on sabbatical leave to study Plato and Aristotle at King's College; the other (1905-1906) on an exchange professorship at the Sorbonne. In all, the roving philosopher made 38 transatlantic crossings.

The wanderer was restless in his confinement at Harvard. He liked to study, but despised teaching. In his only, but very successful, novel, his confused hero became a teacher "because he couldn't do anything else." Oliver, in *The Last Puritan*, speaks for his creator when he says: "People must teach themselves or remain ignorant, and the latter was what the majority preferred." [19] Santayana looked upon teaching as a means to make a living, and to finance his journeys abroad. From the beginning, he saved for his anticipated retirement. "In reality," he said, "I was always out of my element in teaching and in society, and was saying something forced." [20]

His pedagogical method was to expose a literary history of philosophy, believing that "philosophy can be communicated only by being evoked." He declared that "the history of philosophy is the only philosophy that should be taught in a university. Systems of philosophy are taught only by sects or by individuals setting out to be prophets and to found a sect." [21] Hence he merely presented, eclectically, the particular persons and ideas selected, and stimulated class discussion. He deprecated his own ability as a popular or profound teacher, describing his lectures as "desultory, not rich in information, and not well arranged for taking notes." [22] His students, however, judged differently. Others have described the spontaneous applause of students at the close of his lectures, the enjoyment and intellectual stimulation he provided them. [23]

He preferred the company of his students rather than his fellow-professors. He was a bachelor and delighted in considering himself a perpetual student. He dined at their clubs, lived in their dormitories. He even enjoyed watching their football games and practice sessions. This indulgence in the joyful spirit of youth relieved the tedium and aloofness of his academic life. He was not popular with the faculty or the administration. While he always spoke kindly of them, they did not reciprocate. William James was known to have made personal, derogatory remarks, at least in later years; and he took occasion in reviewing a book of Santayana's to heap scorn on the latter's philosophical tenets. Santayana knew that he was disliked by President Eliot; the feeling was mutual. He considered Eliot an anti-humanist who saw in education only a means to ultimate service in the world of big business. He said:

> My relations with President Eliot and with other influential persons had always been strained. I had disregarded or defied public opinion by not becoming a specialist, but writing pessimistic, old-fashioned verses, continuing to range superficially over literature and philosophy, being indiscernibly a Catholic or an atheist, attacking Robert Browning, prophet of the half-educated and half-believing, avoiding administrative duties, neglecting the intelligentsia, frequenting the society of undergraduates and fashionable ladies, spending my holidays abroad, and even appearing as a witness in the disreputable Russell trial.[24]

The increasing emphasis on specialization at Harvard irked Santayana, who favored a humanistic, liberal education. This distasteful trend evoked one of his bitterest comments when he later described the faculty as "an anonymous concourse of coral insects, each secreting one cell, and leaving that fossil legacy to enlarge the earth." [25]

The breach was widening and the decisive break was near. With only himself to support, living simply, almost austerely, he was able to accumulate a savings fund that would provide an early retirement. He was delivering occasional lectures at other colleges, both in New England and in the midwest. Besides, he had begun to write for publication and increasing royalties promised future security.

His entrance into the publication field was the result of a course he gave on aesthetics to clear his own mind on the subject. "I didn't have then," he later admitted, "and haven't now, a clear notion of what 'aesthetics' may be. . . ." [26] After giving what he called this "sham course" for two years, he wrote out the substance of it in book form under the title *The Sense of Beauty*. The manuscript made the rounds of the publishers until at last Scribner's agreed to print it. The sale was modest and the critical reaction unenthusiastic. But Santayana had found a new outlet, a more extensive medium of expression, and a less restrictive means of livelihood. Later he wrote a small book of *Interpretations of Religion and Poetry*, in which he concluded that "religion was poetry intervening in life." A book of poetry followed, and then a five-volume work based on his Philosophy of History course, entitled *The Life of Reason*. This last work insured his literary success, and gained for him prestige in philosophical circles.

His habitual discontent, combined with an encouraging literary success, hastened his self-imposed expatriation. Until the end of his life he could say that he never lost the sense of being a stranger, always on the outside of everything looking in, always alone. This sentiment, so persistent and pervading, nourished his natural preference for solitude. He wrote:

> As for me, not only my body but my rather special and difficult relations to persons and places seemed clearly imposed facts; and in that setting my personal tastes and feelings became apparent, and caused me to feel that I lived in a kind of solitude—not transcendental and spiritual, but decidedly solitariness in a crowd and foreignness among very distinct people. My preferences were already marked and out of harmony with my surroundings and, as I soon felt, with my times. But conceit, or firmness of disposition, kept me from suspecting that I ought to change my allegiances, and think,

THE MIND OF SANTAYANA

and feel, play and work, as did the majority. Nor did I feel
any impulse to contradict them or blame them. I had nothing
to complain of, but I preferred solitude.[27]

There is a romantic legend to the effect that during class
one day Santayana looked out of the window, turned to
his students saying "I have a date with spring" and strode
out of the classroom never to return again. He denied that
there was any foundation to this oft-told tale. Rather, in
January, 1912, at the mid-term, he made his considered request and obtained his release from teaching duties. Feeling
a fresh lease on life, he shaved the beard he had affected
and took a boat for Europe. In London he received news
of his mother's death. There was nothing left to keep him
in America. He never returned again to the United States.
Santayana described the new phase of his life:

> The last echoes of my official career were posthumous: the
> professor was dead, the man revived, spoke in the professor's
> place, and spoke in England. These were all written lectures,
> and most of them were published in *Character and Opinion
> in the United States.* Together with *Egotism in German Phi-
> losophy* and *Soliloquies in England,* they mark my emancipa-
> tion from official control and professional pretensions. There
> was no occasion to change my subjects, to abandon even tech-
> nical philosophy or my interest in academic life and the hu-
> manities. But all was now a voluntary study, a satirical survey,
> a free reconsideration: the point of view had become at once
> frankly personal and speculatively transcendental. A spirit, the
> spirit in a stray individual, was settling its accounts with the
> universe. My official career had happily come to an end.[28]

He was in London when the war broke out. For the sake
of safety and seclusion he retired to Oxford during these
years. Here, he says, "in spite of the war then raging, fancy
in me had taken a new lease of life." [29] He wrote reflective
and skillfully-styled essays for periodicals, and occasionally
lectured. There was no feverish schedule to meet, no un-

pleasant duties to fulfill. He was surrounded by the frenzy of war. "Yet," he said, "nature and solitude continued to envelop me in gentleness, and seemed to remain nearer to me than all that was near." [30]

He seemed reconciled to his earlier repudiation of supernatural faith. He said: ". . . the enlightened Catholic . . . in leaving the church, has merely rediscovered God, finding him now not in the church alone, but in the church only as an expression of human fancy, and in human life itself only as in one out of myriad forms of natural existence." [31] He substituted for God a nameless "Mother Nature."

During these middle years he could and did indulge his fancy in his selected solitude. Out of it, in time, was born his own system of philosophy, expressed, by way of introduction, in *Scepticism and Animal Faith,* and elaborated later in the four volumes of *Realms of Being.* His solitude and introspection gradually assumed the proportions of a spiritual discipline and a way of life. Speaking of solitude, he called it:

> . . . the sole path to happiness for the intellectual man, because [he] cannot be satisfied with a world of perpetual change, defeat and imperfection. It is the path trodden by ancient philosophers and modern poets and saints; not of course by modern writers on philosophy (except Spinoza), because they have not been philosophers in the vital sense; they have practiced no spiritual discipline. . . .[32]

He recognized two sources of this cult of solitude, one a primitive seminal slumber, the other the flight of imagination. "For beneath natural society," he wrote, "in the heart of each of its members, there is always an intense and jealous solitude, the sleep of elemental life which can never be wholly broken; and above natural society there is always another solitude—a placid ethereal wilderness, the heaven of ideas—beckoning the mind." [33]

He stayed in England four years, until the Armistice. He liked the Englishman's "contentment in finitude, fair outward ways, manly perfection and simplicity." [34] Elsewhere he described his ethnic model more concretely: "The Englishman does in a distinguished way the simple things that other men might slur over as unimportant." [35]

The years following the first World War found Santayana traveling around Europe, settling either in Rome or Paris, with occasional visits to England and Spain. A friend of these later years recalls him "in the green setting of the Pincio in April, or sitting in a cafe on the Champs-Élysées in June, with the sun slipping behind the Arc de Triomphe." [36] Meanwhile his prolific pen turned out more books and articles. His own favorite work, produced during this period and written in a medium best suited to his flair for fancy, was *Dialogues in Limbo*. During this same period he finished *Realms of Being*, completing the full exposition of his philosophical doctrine.

He was in Rome at the beginning of World War II. Advanced in age and suffering ill health, he needed personal care and assurance of final security. He abandoned hotel life and found final refuge in a small hospital on one of the seven hills of the Eternal City. There, under the familial care of the "Blue Sisters" of the Little Company of Mary, he retired to a single modest room at the far end of a quiet wing. He had his books, and for a while he continued to write.

He read the Bible through and then wrote a book called *The Idea of Christ in the Gospels*, concerning himself only with the human aspiration to divinity, the idea of the divine in man. He pretended no interest in historical or literal interpretations, but he clearly indicated his conviction that all of Sacred Scripture was the product of purely human and poetic inspiration. Another volume, *Dominations and Powers*, appeared in his 88th year. This was a rambling series of essays on politics, reminiscent of Plato's *Republic*.

During the last year of his life his faculties were failing him. A cataract had developed in one eye, and sight in both of them was impaired. He had to use a magnifying glass to read, and even then it was an effort. His hearing gradually diminished; the strain and embarrassment occasioned by visitors forced him to restrict his hospitality. Eating was painful because of the cancer that gnawed at his stomach. In distress, he could give very little attention to the abridged revision of his *Life of Reason*, and left most of the work to his secretary.

The final decade of his life had been a realization of the ultimate detachment he desired, and thus described:

> I have ultimately become a sort of hermit, not from fear or horror of mankind, but by sheer preference for peace and obscurity. Fortune has become indifferent to me, except as fortune might allow me to despise fortune and to live simply in some beautiful place. I have cut off all superficial society, reducing it to the limits of sincere friendship or intellectual sympathy. . . . I am happy in solitude and confinement, and the furious factions into which the world is divided inspire hatred for none of them in my heart.[37]

But the final year of that decade of satisfying detachment was painful, morally as well as physically. On his 88th birthday he told reporters: "I find things are not so simple to explain as I had imagined, and so I am not reconciled." [38]

Still unreconciled, he died on Friday, Sept. 26, 1952. Characteristically, he had requested that he be buried "in neutral [unconsecrated] ground in a Catholic cemetery."

Chapter Two

Philosophical Background

TO RETRACE the formative steps of an eclectic philosopher, and discover the sources of the many ingredients that have gone into his heterogeneous synthesis, is a tremendous and perhaps impossible task. An investigator can, of course, limit himself to an examination of a few basic sources of certain dominant themes in the philosophy of his subject. C. J. Sullivan has done this in his treatment of "Santayana's Philosophical Inheritance."[1] In this brief article he touches upon the more obvious sources of Santayana's materialism, Platonism, and scepticism.

Another less restrictive and more comprehensive approach is possible. Aided by Santayana's personal reflections, abundant in his philosophical works as well as his memoirs, we can note the particular philosophers he has encountered in his studies, especially in the classroom as a student and as a professor, and observe his expressed reactions and impressions.

Following such a method, however, we cannot hope for a complete or an accurate report. The modern mind, conceived eclectically, is a bastard child that cannot readily recognize his own parents, or refuses to recognize them. The philosophical heritage of George Santayana is not an easy matter to pin down to precise particulars. The best one can do is to refrain from arbitrary judgments, let the man speak for himself, and take him at his word as he gives an account of his philosophical history.

Keeping in mind those preliminary influences of family and faith which strongly impressed his sensitive temperament, we can begin with Santayana's first formal encounter with philosophy at Harvard. The two most prominent professors during that period at Harvard were William James, a pragmatic empiricist, and Josiah Royce, an idealist. Santayana studied under both of them.

He preferred James to Royce, both for doctrine and presentation, although he enjoyed the speculative play of Royce's idealistic dialectic. He was reticent, however, about attributing any strong influence to James. There may be a personal reason for this, since they were on the faculty together later on and found themselves far apart in their philosophical and personal tastes.

Santayana mentions some of the courses he took under James: one on Taine's *De l'Intelligence*, another an exposition of the doctrines of Locke, Berkeley and Hume, a third a study of Spencer. But from these he claims he was "not conscious of any intellectual residuum" and seemed "to have gathered no clear lesson from those authors or from James himself." [2] In one instance he credited some enlightenment from the early medical psychology of James. During his graduate study he sat in on a seminar in which James read the manuscript of his *Principles of Psychology*. Of this seminar he said:

> Even then what I learned from him was perhaps chiefly things which he explicitly never taught, but which I imbibed from the spirit and background of his teaching. Chief of these, I should say, was a sense for the immediate: for the unadulterated, unexplained, instant fact of experience. [3]

He admired the natural boldness that James displayed, but that same trait of temperament expressed later on in pragmatic philosophy repelled him. Speaking of the appearance of James' *Pragmatism*, Santayana said: "I could not stomach that way of speaking about truth. . . . The William James who had been my master was not this William James of the later years, whose pragmatism and pure empiricism and romantic metaphysics have made such a stir in the world." [4]

Santayana likewise attributed little influence to Royce, whom he succeeded in the chair of philosophy. He took an early dislike towards the dialectic of the German idealists, and Royce was an exponent of that intricate and ethereal system that enshrined an Absolute in thought. Said Santayana:

> Royce had a powerful and learned mind, and it was always profitable, if not pleasant, to listen to him; not pleasant because his voice was harsh, his style heavy, repetitious and pedantic, and his monotonous preoccupation with his own system intolerable. To listen was profitable, nevertheless, because his comfortless dissatisfaction with every possible idea opened vistas and disturbed a too easy dogmatism: while the perversity and futility of his dialectic threw one back in the end on the great certainties and the great possibilities, such as made the minds of the great philosophers at once sublime and sane. [5]

Under James, Santayana took a course in the philosophy of Herbert Spencer, with whom he claimed no affinity. Yet at the end of the first volume of his *Psychology*, Spencer remarked that it did not matter what explanations of the universe were postulated as its principles, since terms are only symbols pointing at some unknowable reality. Such pure nominalism smacks strongly of Santayana's own. He said, however:

> Herbert Spencer, I think, taught me nothing. I agreed with his naturalism or materialism, because that is what we all start with: the minimum presupposition of perception and action. But I agreed with James about Spencer's theory of evolution:

It was a tangle of words, of loose generalities that some things might sometimes suggest to us, and that, said properly, it might have been witty to say, but that had absolutely no value as "laws" or "causes" of events. Such "principles" might serve an "objective idealist," not a naturalist or a scientific man. . . . Spencer, unlike Lucretius and Spinoza, had no speculative power. He meant to be a naturalist, but language and hypostasized ideas of progress turned him into an idealistic metaphysician.[6]

It was through a Latin course, not a philosophy course, that the undergraduate Santayana found and fed upon a source that nourished the primary postulate of his own philosophy. He had heard his father quote with gusto from Lucretius. In an advanced Latin course taken at Harvard, he read for himself the bard of Epicurean materialism. He learned, he said, "the great passages by heart."

Even the physical and biological theories seemed instructive, not as scientific finalities, if science could be final, but as serving to dispel the notion that anything is non-natural or miraculous. If the theory suggested were false, another no less naturalistic would be true: and this presumption recommended itself to me and has become one of my first principles: not that a particular philosophy called naturalism must be true *a priori*, but that nature sets the standard of naturalness.[7]

Having rejected the supernatural in his adolescent conflict with religion, the young philosopher needed allies and welcomed the crude materialism of a tragic poet who flavored his bitter philosophic food with spicy flights of fancy and served it with skillful metrical composition. Santayana also needed corroboration of his own fanciful perspective of historical facts and reasonable conclusions, an elevation of imagination over intellect. He found it in the romantic approach to history:

· 31 ·

There was one lesson, however, which I was readier to learn, not only at Harvard from Professor Palmer and afterwards at Berlin from Paulsen, but from the general temper of that age well represented for me by the *Revue Des Deux Mondes* (which I habitually read from cover to cover) and by the works of Taine and of Matthew Arnold—I refer to the historical spirit of the nineteenth century, and to that splendid panorama of nations and religions, literatures and arts, which it unrolled before the imagination.[8]

The single philosopher to whom Santayana acknowledges his greatest debt, and to whom he gives unstinted praise, is Benedict de Spinoza, whom he first studied under Royce. Santayana was attracted to Spinoza's concept of dynamic matter and his naturalistic god of infinite substance. Even more appealing was the doctrine of natural morality. There was a personal affinity as well. Spinoza also had turned from orthodox faith to naturalistic speculation in solitude. "I will not attempt," said Santayana, "to describe here the lessons that I learned in the study of Spinoza, lessons that in several respects laid the foundation of my philosophy." [9] He went on to explain his enthusiasm for Spinoza's naturalistic ethics:

As I have said elsewhere, I regard Spinoza as the only modern philosopher in the line of orthodox physics, the line that begins with Thales and culminates, for Greek philosophy, in Democritus. Orthodox physics should inspire and support orthodox ethics; and perhaps the chief source of my enthusiasm for Spinoza has been the magnificent clearness of his orthodoxy on this point. Morality is something natural. It arises and varies, not only psychologically but prescriptively and justly, with the nature of the creature whose morality it is.[10]

Other philosophers studied by Santayana during his undergraduate days were: Descartes, Leibniz, Hobbes, Mandeville, and John Stuart Mill. The nominalism and sensism of Hobbes appealed to the budding philosopher. He credited Hobbes with a principle borrowed: "Hobbes had said . . . 'No discourse whatsoever can end in absolute knowledge of fact; and I have made the *authority of things*,* as against the presumption of words or ideas, a principle of my philosophy.' " [11] This is a particularly meaningless expression, for things are mute and the mind must form ideas and consequently words about them if we are to accept their evidence and speak at all.

During his graduate years at Berlin, he ran the gamut of the German idealists. Although he later denounced their egotism (in a volume opportunely published in America and England in 1916, and again in 1941) [12] he did not pass through them unscathed. He expressed his dislike for their cosmic projection of ideas: "The articulation of knowledge occupies them; and yet, by the hocus-pocus of metaphysics, they substitute this human experience for the whole universe in which it rises." [13]

Their transcendental method, however, appealed to him and gave him directions beyond his materialism. James and Royce had not offered much help on the mind-versus-matter problem. Santayana found a supposed solution in oscillation: ". . . it was only afterwards, when I read Fichte and Schopenhauer, that I began to see my way to a solution. We must oscillate between a radical transcendentalism, frankly reduced to a solipsism of the living moment, and a materialism posited as a presupposition of conventional sanity." [14]

In Schopenhauer, he said: "I was able to discount the language of a system and perceive from what direction it drew its inspiration. The 'Will' in Schopenhauer was a transparent mythological symbol for the flux of matter. There was absolute equivalence between such a system, in its purport and sense for reality, and the systems of Spinoza and Lucretius. This was the element of ancient sanity that kept me awake

* Unless otherwise indicated, all italics within quotations are original and not imposed.

and conscious of the points of the compass in the subsequent wreck of psychologism." [15]

In Berlin, he also studied Kant's *Critique of Pure Reason*, as well as some Indian philosophy. He inveighed against Kant's uncritical criticism as a forging of artificial categories, assuming "that mind everywhere must have a single grammar" and so rigorously imposing those categories "that people supposed he was establishing the sciences on a solid foundation, rather than prescribing for all men a gratuitious uniformity in error." [16] This was a bitter denunciation in the mouth of a man who unhesitatingly used Kant's fatal transcendentalism and consequently reduced all science to sheer symbolism! Indian philosophy, on the other hand, strongly attracted him because of its mystical elements and its pure transcendental reflection which does not attempt to return to reality with a filing case of categories.

His doctorate dissertation was a critical study of the philosophy of Hermann Lotze. In reflection, he quickly passed over the subject of his dissertation, saying: "Lotze was stillborn, and I have forgotten everything that I then had to read in him and to ponder." [17] Lotze, however, had eliminated abstraction as a real representation of essences; and Santayana's nominalism disparaged abstraction in the same way. He would have preferred, he said, to do his dissertation on Hegel. "I liked Hegel's *Phaenomenologie;* it set me planning my *Life of Reason;* and now I like even his *Logik,* not the dialectical sophistry in it, but the historical and critical lights that appear by the way. I could have written, even then, a critical thesis, say on *Logic, Sophistry and Truth in Hegel's Philosophy.* This would have knit my own doctrine together at the beginning of my career, as I have scarcely had the chance of doing at the end." [18]

Santayana's familiarity with Hegel is evident. In Santayana's mature system of philosophy there are marked similarities: for example, to Hegel's notion of essence, his division of philosophy according to the idea in-itself, the idea outside-itself, and the idea for-itself; especially to Hegel's notion of the origin of religion in poetry. Santayana was far more indebted to the German idealists than he realized, or cared to admit.

During his teaching career at Harvard, he reviewed what he had learned and deepened his understanding of his philosophical forefathers. He taught James' old course on Locke, Berkeley and Hume; and another on Descartes, Spinoza and Leibniz. Concerning Berkeley and Hume, he later remarked: "Fichte and Nietzsche, in their fervid arrogance, could hardly outdo the mental impoverishment of Berkeley and Hume in their levity; it had really been a sight for the gods to see one of these undergraduates driving matter out of the universe, whilst the other drove out spirit." [19]

As he taught, Santayana gradually strengthened his own opinions and developed his own philosophy: "I wished to rethink the thoughts of those philosophers, to understand why they took the direction they took, and then to consider the consequences and implications of taking that direction. At bottom, I was always discovering and developing my own philosophy." [20]

He thought that Descartes was inconsistent by not carrying his scepticism far enough. "His mind was not plastic nor mystic enough to be profoundly sceptical. . . . He thus assumed the principle of sufficient reason, a principle for which there is no reason at all. If any idea or maxim were really *a priori* or spontaneous in the human mind, it would be infinitely improbable that it should apply to the facts of nature. . . . That anything exists that may be called 'I,' so that I am not a mere essence, is a thousand times more doubtful, and is often denied by the keenest wits." [21] Here is one of Santayana's frequent and incredible misunderstandings, this

time as to the meaning and origin of the principle of sufficient reason. As for the scepticism, Santayana did carry it
further—to an inert solipsism of the present moment. His
mind was plastic enough to perform such mental gymnastics
more deftly.

A course he gave on "The Philosophy of History" pre-
pared the foundation of one of his major works, the *Life
of Reason*. His interest had turned to the ancients:

> What then most enticed me in philosophy was Plato, and
> I had always had a great respect for Aristotle, especially for
> his *Ethics* and *Politics;* and out of these, with the help of a
> glance at Bacon, Locke, Montesquieu, and Taine . . . I com-
> posed my lectures on the "philosophy of history," which for
> me meant no providential plan of creation or redemption, but
> merely retrospective politics; a study of what had formed the
> chief interests of mankind in various epochs.[22]

His interest in Plato and Aristotle, especially the former,
encouraged him to take a sabbatical year at King's College
in Cambridge where he studied them more extensively. In
his writings, however, he supplies little evidence of any extensive reading in, or profound understanding of, Aristotle.
The following year at Harvard he began a series of lectures
on the *Republic*, the *Phaedrus*, the *Symposium*, the *Phaedo*,
and the *Nichomean Ethics*.

When he spoke of his preference for the Greek philosophers, Santayana referred to the natural philosophy of Democritus and the moral philosophy of Plato. He acknowledged his debt to them in the formation of his own philosophy: "Both the Greeks and Spinoza, by a spontaneous
agreement, combined the two insights that for me were essential: naturalism as to the origin and history of mankind,
and fidelity, in moral sentiment, to the inspiration of reason,
by which the human mind conceives truth and eternity, and
participates in them ideally." [23]

The major figures of Greek philosophy, Plato and Aristotle, he admired from a distance and with considerable reservation. Having settled on transcendentalism and nominalism, he was impatient with Aristotle's metaphysics and his psychology of abstraction. He was even more impatient with logical argumentation. Plato offered him some interesting moral insights, and surely Plato's theory of ideas influenced Santayana's notion of essence. But he blamed Plato for, what seemed to him, giving cosmic power to apotheosized forms; and for restricting eternal forms to universals and not seeing the absolute character of every particular. He generally protested that "the Greeks [beginning with Socrates] . . . were rhetoricians. They seldom or never reverted to the immediate for a foothold in thought . . . they were disputatious, and in that sense no opinion escaped their criticism." [24]

Influenced by Cartesian dualism and Kantian transcendentalism, with their consequent denial of immediate access to reality, Santayana saw in metaphysics only an arbitrary verbal transcript, made by the mind from its own stuffing, and foisted upon nature. "Metaphysics," he said, "is not merely speculative physics . . . anticipating what might some day be discovered. This is what the naturalists had done, and their theories were simply physical or cosmological. But after Socrates a theory constructed by reasoning, in terms of logic, ethics, and a sort of poetic propriety, was put in the place of physics; the economy of the human mind was projected into the universe; and nature, in the works of the metaphysicians, held the mirror up to man." [25]

In the philosophy of Henri Bergson, according to Santayana the only great philosopher he knew personally, there are some points of similarity to Santayana's doctrine: the flux of matter warring against the spirit, the prejudice of intellect in interpreting that flux, the preference of intuition which alone can grasp the essences of things. Santayana especially delighted in Bergson's notion of what he called *La fonction fabulatrice*, the creative function of the imagination that is capable of supplying all that a man needs and lacks in reality. For Santayana, who had decided that revelation was a product of poetic inspiration and had relegated religion to the realm of fancy, this Bergsonian notion was a comforting concept. But it was discomforting for him to learn that Bergson, some time before his death, had professed belief in Catholic doctrine and had requested baptism.

Concluding Santayana's own comments on his philosophical heritage, a summary can be made in his own words: "The first philosophers, the original observers of life and nature, were the best; and I think only the Indians and the Greek naturalists, together with Spinoza, have been right on the chief issue, the relation of man and of his spirit to the universe." [26]

With occasional interjections, too pertinent to suppress, Santayana has been allowed to speak for himself in tracing his philosophical lineage. This is not the proper place or time to make any conclusive critical judgments; but some other summary notions and comments may help to complete the history.

Nothing has been said, for example, about a Thomistic, or generally Scholastic, influence in Santayana's philosophical history. But he gives no evidence, expressed or implied, of such an influence. He has said that when he entered Harvard he was "already alive to the fundamental questions, and even had a certain dialectical nimbleness, due to familiarity with the fine points of theology"; consequently he referred to his "Scholastic logic." [27] There is no evidence in his life, however, of any theological training, unless his reference is to his childhood study of the catechism and his attendance at some Catholic sermons during his early youth. And in spite of its high secondary school rating, it is doubtful that

Boston Latin School, even in its most creditable years, offered courses in Scholastic logic. Occasionally he mentioned with admiration the "dialectical pungency" of St. Thomas Aquinas; but he gave no indication of any serious study of the works of the Angelic Doctor. Reasoned arguments were alien to his fanciful spirit; and he supposed all forms of argumentation, syllogistic demonstrations included, to be rhetorical dialectic. He did indulge in Scholastic terminology. But he borrowed these terms from the Aristotelian tradition and gave them altogether different meanings according to his own intent. He wrote:

> I am a Scholastic at heart, but I lack the patience and the traditional training that might have enabled me to discuss every point minutely, without escapades or ornament or exaggeration or irony. My books would then have been much more solid, and nobody would have read them. For better or for worse, I am a Scholastic only in my principles not in my ways. I detest disputation and distrust, proofs and disproofs.[28]

This is a candid admission, but one which unfortunately puts the professed philosopher in the position of an anti-intellectual. Santayana's own life of reason was much more a life of imagination.

The main streams of philosophical thought which flowed into his own system were those that watered the budding philosophy already in him when he entered Harvard and began his formal studies. He looked for confirmation of that naturalism, or originative materialism, which he frankly referred to as a "presupposition" and a "first principle." Having rejected the supernatural personally, he sought justification philosophically. Hence his early seizure of the crude naturalism of the early Greeks, poetically presented—and thus appealing to his aesthetic temperament—by Lucretius.

But this same aesthetic temperament, so familiar with the realm of spirit, could not tolerate a restricted materialism that could not provide for spiritual insights and moral harmony. For these, he went to Plato, a lover of ideal forms, like himself, and to Spinoza, a kindred suffering soul, who could offer an aloof and unobtrusive god in capitalized Nature, and a soothing natural morality as well. Anyone else who could bolster either side of this dualism was acceptable.

When a man has firmly fixed his position with regard to the fundamental questions, he can find ample support for that position in the history of philosophy. There is range enough of conflicting opinions in the record of human speculation to provide props for any conceivable point of view; that is, as long as a man despises disputation and distrusts proofs and disproofs. And so Santayana could, and did, scribble marginalia on his copy of Lucretius and identify the poet's term *notitia* with his own "animal faith," and decide that when Berkeley spoke of "notion" he really meant to say "object of intent." So, too, he could, and did, preface each book of the *Realms of Being* with a list of heterogeneous quotations from diverse philosophers as indications of some vague agreement with his own doctrine.

Nor was Santayana a man to be dislodged from his position, since his epiphenomenalism forbade him to acknowledge any reasonable demonstration; he preferred trust in "intuition" or "insight" according to the play of his imagination. In his selected solitude he gave free rein to a vivid imagination; from it came his notion of essence and its primacy in thought and life. This was the source of the sheer essentialism of his philosophy.

All that was needed was a public occasion for the formal debut of his notion of essence. The occasion was the epistemological controversy that gave rise to the school of Critical Neo-Realism.

Chapter Three

Critical Neo-Realism

THE directions taken by most modern philosophers have their source in the dichotomy imposed by Descartes between mind and matter, a gulf opened by sceptical subjectivism and widened by Kant's transcendentalism. Two divergent paths were followed by their short-sighted successors: one leading to sensism and positivism, favored in England and France; the other, preferred in Germany, led to pure rationalism and idealism.

The dialectical extremes of Fichte, Hegel and Schelling disintegrated into the irrationalism of Schopenhauer and Nietzsche. There followed a distrust of reason and an emphasis on affective development through vital evolution. Then, favored by the historical studies of the latter part of the last century, a neo-Kantian movement gained momentum. By the turn of this century a still undefined materialism clashed with a revived idealism; between the two rose the unlaid specter of "the critical problem," which for many was the only problem in philosophy. This obsession was perhaps justified, because, without the assurance of man's power to transcend himself to reach reality, all philosophy, indeed all science, could be nothing but mere supposition and surmise, a conclusion with which many philosophers were content.

America, still too young for an indigenous culture, busy with her building and commerce, simply echoed the current philosophical parlance of her learned cousins across the sea:

She accepted the British influence of Locke and Berkeley until the Revolution; then, changing her philosophical as well as her political allegiance, she reiterated the dogmas of the French rationalists and deists; but during the nineteenth century the romantic temperament of her youth changed her philosophical affection to German sentimentalism and idealism.

At the beginning of the present century, America was ready to develop a native philosophical movement; it took the vigorous form of a new realism. She was not independent in her venture; for a renewed commercial alliance with England involved an ideological exchange that effected a simultaneous development in philosophy.

Neo-Realism represented a combined reaction in England and in America against the revival of idealism. Generally speaking, it was a direct turnabout: an over-simplified reduction of all reality to physical nature, as opposed to the idealistic reduction of all reality to psychic contents. With overtones of materialism, the Neo-Realists attempted to explain mind and spirit through purely natural processes and physical laws. The trend toward realism was initiated in Germany by Franz Brentano and Alexius Meinong, followed by Edmund Husserl. But it was in England and America that the trend developed into maturity, with the strength and force to overthrow and expel idealism.

In England, as the century and the philosophical tide turned, idealism, in various forms, was represented by Stirling and Green, John and Edward Caird, and F. H. Bradley; later figures included J. S. Mackenzie, J. M. E. McTaggert and James Ward. G. E. Moore is recognized as the first strong exponent of realism in England. In his essay, "The Refutation of Idealism" (1903), Moore insisted upon the independence of extra-mental reality and appealed to the distinction between the object sensed and the act of sensation, or psychic awareness. S. S. Alexander, in *Space, Time, and Deity* (1920), attempted a realistic metaphysic, postulating space-time as the matrix of reality. Bertrand Russell, in his *Analysis of Mind* (1921), proposed the notion of a world "stuff" of "neutral particulars," which, in varying context, make both mind and matter; in certain patterns they produce psychic states. By 1925, when he began his Harvard lectures, A. N. Whitehead had published *Science and the Modern World*, expressing his philosophy of organism which centered upon actual experience, a metaphysic of concrete reality.

Other exponents of realism in England, though differing in their expressions of it, were: L. T. Hobhouse and, later, C. D. Broad, John Laird, Lloyd Morgan and P. T. Nunn. During the ascendancy of realism and the decline of idealism, Cambridge University espoused the new trend, while Oxford clung to the older tradition.

Neo-Realism was an earlier and a more vigorous movement in the United States. The die-hard idealists of the period were: W. T. Harris, founder of *The Journal of Speculative Philosophy*, G. H. Howison of the University of California, Mary W. Calkins of Wellesley College, Borden P. Bowne of Boston University, Harvard's Josiah Royce, and G. T. Ladd and James E. Creighton. It was the revolt of two former students of Royce that prompted the organized rise of realism. One of these rebels credited the pragmatism of William James and the instrumentalism of John Dewey with paving the way out of intellectual monism towards a realistic pluralism.[1]

Royce, in the first volume of his *Gifford Lectures*, had attacked the stirring spirit of realism. William P. Montague, a professor at Columbia University, retaliated with an article in *The Philosophical Review* (March, 1901), in which he counterattacked "Professor Royce's Refutation of Realism."

Ralph B. Perry, teaching at Harvard, where he, too, had formerly studied under Royce, followed with another rebuttal in *The Monist* (Oct., 1901), "Professor Royce's Refutation of Realism and Pluralism."

In 1910, six champions of the new realism formed an organized group to promote their doctrine. These were: Professors R. B. Perry and E. B. Holt of Harvard, W. T. Marvin and E. G. Spaulding of Princeton, W. B. Pitkin and W. P. Montague of Columbia. Their first combined effort appeared in that same year, an article published in *The Journal of Philosophy* entitled "A Program and Platform of Six Realists." Two years later they published a co-operative volume, *The New Realism*. Many other American professors of philosophy followed their lead, without joining their organization.

The members of this pioneering group differed widely in their metaphysical views, but they agreed on certain methodological and epistemological postulates. These were:

1. *Following the example of scientists, philosophers should co-operate in a critical exchange of their views.* (This method was put into practice through seminars at which individual members read reports of their findings; but Montague admits it was not wholly successful, often degenerating into a tacit agreement of "I'll pass your stuff if you'll pass mine." [2])

2. *Like scientists, they should isolate and work out particular problems.* (They focused their attention on the epistemological problem and agreed in general to the realistic principle that "knowledge as such makes no difference to the objects known.")

3. *Some, at least, of the particulars of which we are conscious exist when we are not conscious of them—existential realism.*

4. *Some, at least, of the essences or universals subsist when we are not conscious of them—subsistential realism.*

5. *Some, at least, of these particulars and universals that are real are apprehended directly, rather than indirectly through copies or mental images—presentative realism.*

Neo-Realism, then, attacked the foundations of idealism: subjectivism, the identification of the external object with the apprehension of that object; and universalism, the postulate of an Absolute (presuming that diversity is phenomenal and unity noumenal), in which all oppositions and distinctions are resolved. The philosophers of Neo-Realism, adhering to the restricted approach of empiricism, denied any postulate that reality was systematic and rejected any *a priori* macrocosmic principle. They considered the philosopher's task to be mere speculation on general problems proposed by particular physical sciences, resulting in nothing more than hypotheses about fragments of reality encountered in experience.

The argument for existential realism, proposed especially by Perry in his essay on "The Egocentric Predicament," refuted the presumption of idealism that the necessary conjunction of consciousness with its object in sensation implied an identity of the two. This presumptive and fallacious principle, he concluded, rested on sheer tautology. Consciousness is not the sole datum but only an essential part of the whole cognitional process. The argument for subsistential realism was made along the same lines. Consciousness, in every instance, is selective rather than constitutive, and the objects themselves can be explained in terms of external rather than internal relations.

Here, too, the Neo-Realists parted company with the pragmatists. Pragmatism would admit an ontological truth only by its logical verification in experience. The idealists had used the "egocentric predicament" to challenge a knowledge of reality apart from conscious experience; the pragmatists used the same fallacious predicament to deny the truth of a thing aside from experiential judgment. With keener insight, the Neo-Realists perceived that the ontological truth or falsity of a judgment, as well as its independent existence, antedates its verification or refutation in judicative experience. In other words, the simple fact so clear to common sense: that which exists is discovered and not created by the act of cognition; in creatures, ontological truth does not depend on logical truth but vice versa.

Hence idealism correctly held to the absolute character of truth, while incorrectly holding to an idealistic monism. Pragmatism was properly pluralistic, but wrongly assigned a relative criterion of truth. Neo-Realism, on the other hand, sought the middle road on the route to reality. The Neo-Realists, however, failed to conceive the ontological and transcendental character of the good, agreeing with the pragmatists in making value "relative to the needs and satisfactions of individuals."

Furthermore, they failed to achieve an adequate approach to realism: the Neo-Realists by their monistic materialism, their successors, the Critical Neo-Realists, by their inexplicable and exaggerated dualism.

Among themselves, the Neo-Realists were not agreed in their epistemological expositions. Perry and Holt were opposed in their views to that held by Montague. Pitkin, Marvin and Spaulding were wavering fellow-travelers, agreeing with the general trend towards realism but never clear as to which side they were on in the disagreement which ensued between their more articulate confreres.

Perry and Holt held for a mechanistic and behavioristic explanation, reducing conscious awareness to a "specific response," a wholly physical reaction of the nervous system. Any object, they said, insofar as it stimulates cognition is an idea; but independently, and in relation to other things, it is a physical object without relations internal to the knowing subject. This actually amounted to an identity between a thing and the idea of it, denying even a physical medium to cognitional activity.

Furthermore, the Perry-Holt theory proposed a "Relativistic Objectivism," which attributed objective existence to whatever is subjectively apprehended in any particular person's consciousness. In other words, if a sober man sees a policeman with one head, and a drunken man sees the same figure with two heads, then objectively the poor policeman has one head and two heads—yet not three heads, unless some deranged subject experiences such a sight!

Montague quickly perceived that his colleagues had betrayed their espoused cause and were right back to the subjective phenomenalism of Hume and Mill. He pointed out the absurdity of equating the physical response of the organism with the extra-mental object. An organic response is a physical motion, requiring direction and flux. How could such a motion constitute consciousness? It does not even resemble motion, nor can it be directed to an object unless the object of consciousness were present in space. The requirement of a contemporaneous spatial object would fail to explain our apprehension of secondary qualities, abstract ideas, other minds, or events of the past or the future. Furthermore, physical motion implies a distinct and irrevocable succession of instants, which cannot account for that characteristic of consciousness which Bergson calls "interpenetration," a retentive apprehension of the past and an anticipation of the future in the instant of present consciousness. Montague might have added that the possibility of reflexive cognition, potentially *ad infinitum*, likewise discredits any purely physical explanation of the cognitional act.

These difficulties and others (the subjective character of dreams and illusions, for example) ripped the loosely-knit seams of naive realism and, Montague admits, caused and justified the reactionary rise of Critical Neo-Realism.

If perception is immediately objective, then how explain vivid dreams and convincing flights of fancy? The very possibility of raising the question implies that *de facto* we can and do distinguish the real from the imaginary. Montague recognized this obvious defect in the Perry-Holt theory, noting what he called "the profound *asymmetry* of the relation between the veridical and the illusory objects of perception" since "*the illusory perceptions can be explained by the veridical, whereas the veridical cannot be explained by the illusory.*" [3] He also pointed out the two-fold effect of real objects, objective and subjective, as compared with the sole subjective effect of the illusory in apprehension.

It is to Montague's credit that he not only recognized the deficiencies of his colleagues but that he himself approached the point of solution—without, unfortunately, any sound philosophical principles that could have clarified his position. He realized that there must be an identity achieved between the extra-mental object and the knowing subject; he understood that a purely material explanation, a kind of pan-physicalism, was insufficient to account for cognitional experience; yet he did not see how the addition of a psychical element could avoid a dualism which would lead back to subjective phenomenalism.

The failure of a material explanation of our apprehension of extra-spatial images and ideas, as well as of our power of cognitional reflection, necessitates the presence of an immaterial power capable of assimilating without changing the extramental object. Only a totally immaterial power could completely turn back upon itself. But philosophical preconceptions and presumptions prevented this obvious *sequitur*. Lacking any knowledge, or understanding, of the Aristotelian-Thomistic doctrine of form, and its role in cognition, he arrived at the correct position in the middle of the road, but was compelled to stand there speechless. He acknowledged his loss, saying: "The great Thomistic realism of the Catholics was unfortunately regarded by the non-Catholics as too closely bound up with theological dogmas to be of any significance for secular thought." [4] Unfortunate indeed! The deficient Perry-Holt theory led to further confusion and final despair.

In 1920, seven other philosophers collaborated in publishing a collective work entitled *Essays in Critical Realism*. This new group, with a different approach to realism, was composed of Charles A. Strong of Columbia, A. K. Rogers of Yale, A. O. Lovejoy of Johns Hopkins, R. W. Sellars of Michigan, J. B. Pratt of Williams, Durant Drake of Vassar, and George Santayana of Harvard.

Like their predecessors, they coincided in a realistic approach in epistemology, but in their metaphysics and consequent solutions they followed different directions. They were dissatisfied with the conclusions reached by their predecessors and set out to redefine critically a proper approach to epistemological realism.

Their principal doctrine, according to one of its proponents, was "that knowledge of external things and past events is an interpretation of those objects in terms of understood predicates and does not involve the literal presence of these objects in the field of consciousness of the knower. It is the mediateness of knowledge that is stressed. . . . Critical Realism consists in a movement from the view of knowledge characteristic of naive realism to a more adequate view . . . a reinterpretation of the nature of knowledge is the central feature." [5]

All of these philosophers were agreed on a dualistic rather than monistic epistemology, a re-presentative rather than directly presentative approach to realism. They succeeded in establishing certain fundamental postulates:

1. *There are two genera of entities: (a) material things; and (b) mental states or ideas.*
2. *Ideas alone are given and known immediately, while material things are known mediately by causal inference.*

3. *The inferred material objects are numerically distinct from the immediate data of the mind, and are at least partially different in kind or nature from the latter.*

While the earlier, or naive, realists had erred in the extreme of physically (*secundum esse*) identifying the object with the idea, the Critical Neo-Realists simply revived the old objective dualism. Montague correctly concluded that in the basic tenets of his successors there was nothing new, that it was merely "a restatement of the Epistemological Dualism which is explicit in Locke and Descartes, and implicit in Hobbes, Spinoza, and the other modern philosophers prior to Berkeley." [6]

Emphasis on either side of this parallelism leads to the disaster which had doomed the whole course of modern philosophy since Descartes. Concentration on the supposed inaccessibility of reality leads to scepticism and phenomenalism; obsessesion with an idea, supposedly numerically different from the object it represents, leads to sheer idealism. "Now what, if anything," asks Montague, proposing a fair question, "have the Critical Realists done to mitigate the two sad dialectical sequels to Epistemological Dualism with which our philosophic tradition has made us familiar?" [7]

Nearly all the participants in this trend towards realism were naturalists, holding basic metaphysics that ranged from raw materialism to emergent evolution and pan-psychism. With presumptive principles postulating a self-sufficient and self-explanatory material nature, they inevitably failed to penetrate the mystery of cognition in which, by immaterial power, there can be, and is, a distinction between object and idea without, however, any division.

Agreed on their epistemological dualism, the Critical Neo-Realists were sharply divided in their explanations, particularly with regard to the inferential means they proposed in order to bridge the mind-matter gap.

Lovejoy offered an illative theory, by which we deduce the extra-mental from the conscious datum, an altogether inconsistent appeal to ontological causality. Strong and Drake confused external sensation with imagination, giving the former the constitution of an image produced subjectively. They constructed no bridge to reality. Initially, Strong was enthusiastic about Santayana's notion of "essence," which he called "this precious conception;" but later, recognizing the implicit difficulties involved, his enthusiasm waned.

Pratt unsuccessfully tried to distinguish the "denotation" of a sensation from its "signification," but such a theory demanded the spatial presence of an object in every instance of apprehension; hence he was faced with the same problems that stumped the naive realists. Sellars, by his theory of "interpretation," assigned the role of interpreter to the external senses, granting them the power of self-perception.

No more successful in solving the insoluble epistemological problem, as it was proposed, was Santayana's notion of intuited "essence" and his reduction of knowledge of extramental objects to "animal faith." His contribution was the most anti-intellectual and most despairing of any true knowledge. Yet it was this contribution that gained for him philosophical prestige and encouraged his elaboration of the "precious conception."

Briefly, for it will be extensively exposed and criticized later on, essence, for Santayana, is the eternal character of any datum of consciousness. Since this essence is not in the existential order it cannot be identified with extra-mental reality; although by supposition it can be affirmed of it.

With precipitant enthusiasm, one writer commented: "It makes natural and easy the transition to an outer reality, which is so difficult for copyism, and it maintains the distinction between content and object of knowledge, which is denied by naive realism." [8] But the transition to outer reality was by no means "natural and easy," for it required a pledge of faith; and the relation of content to object of knowledge was a difference, not a distinction.

Santayana's essence was, indeed, a source of dispute among the Critical Neo-Realists themselves. They admitted it was "the one question in our inquiry upon which we have not been able fully to agree." [9] Only three of the seven held that an essence in every case was the true character of the mental existent and was itself non-existent. Nevertheless, the notion of essence dominated the discussion, much to the chagrin of Sellars, who later complained that their work had "directed attention to the doctrine of essence, a doctrine held in its extreme form by an actual minority of the contributors and, even then, not central to Critical Realism." [10]

Disliking disputation (and what, among philosophers, is more disputable than the epistemological problem?) Santayana withdrew from the fray and went his own way to develop his "precious conception." This development required a retreat from "irrational existence," that world which had become for him "ashes in the mouth"—and so in his solitude Santayana cultivated and richly elaborated the keystone of his philosophy, his notion of essence.

Part II—Exposition

I would lay siege to the truth only as animal exploration and
fancy may do so.

GEORGE SANTAYANA
Scepticism and Animal Faith

Introductory Note

On Some Basic Notions in Santayana's Philosophy

BEFORE proceeding to an exposition of Santayana's notion of essence, it will be helpful to examine certain preliminary and fundamental notions which he proposes. What, for example, does he understand by the very term *philosophy?* What role does he assign to *reason* in the study of philosophy? Does he explicitly propose a *system* of philosophy? What does he mean by the fundamental phrase: *realms of being?*

To understand Santayana's approach to philosophy, a basic conclusion must be anticipated: a definite dichotomy lies at the very foundation of his doctrine. The detailed study that follows will show how the initial cleavage was made, and then trace the consequent dualism. One consequence, already contained in the presuppositions he brought to his mature philosophy, is a self-imposed restriction on his investigations. According to himself, the only cognitional paths open to Santayana are: intuition of appearance, or the datum of consciousness; and a blind, instinctive faith in existents as they are encountered in action and anticipation.

He begins to philosophize on this presumption, making his way only by "exploration and fancy." [1]

Philosophy, for Santayana, is a general picture of nature that the human mind composes as it gropes through nature's jungle and grapples with the objects encountered there. It is not a science, "only a balance of mind and temper, in which all the sciences and arts should compose as true a picture as possible of nature and human nature." [2]

Philosophy, therefore, can make no boast of embracing the universe and squeezing out of it a set of well-ordered principles. On the contrary, philosophy is only a means to adjustment, "a harmony among irrational impulses." Even in its proper task, philosophy often fails. "Philosophy is not a useful science, like mathematics, requisite for engineers. It is a remnant or an echo of prophetic inspirations launched in antiquity into an ignorant world, and it perpetuates the Babel there." [3]

Throughout five volumes on the subject, Santayana never proposed a precise definition of reason. He preferred to describe it as a vague mediator between the ideal and the physical, a conscious selection, discrimination, organization, harmony. Reason, he says, "is the happy marriage of two elements—impulse and ideation—which if wholly divorced would reduce man to a brute or a maniac." [4] Reason is a reflective spectator, observing and interpreting the conflicting events of animal life. "The life of reason, as I conceive it, is simply the dreaming mind becoming coherent, devising symbols and methods, such as languages, by which it may fitly survey its own career, and the forces of nature on which that career depends. Reason thereby raises our vegetative dream into a poetic revelation and transcript of truth." [5]

Reason, therefore, is conscious interpretation of nature and events, physical or ideal. Santayana disregarded any distinction between sensate and intellectual knowledge, and fuses all forms of interpretation into the functions of imagination or "fancy." Philosophy, then, is a reflective summary of man's reactions to the world he encounters in action. It embraces all articulate experience, whether expressed in scientific formulas, syllogistic demonstrations, or poetry. Philosophy is life; or, rather, the reflective response to life. Santayana explains:

> I should not give the title of philosopher to every logician or psychologist who, in his official and studious moments, may weigh argument against argument or may devise expedients for solving theoretical puzzles. I see no reason why a philosopher should be puzzled. What he sees he sees; of the rest he is ignorant, and his sense of this vast ignorance (which is his natural and inevitable condition) is a chief part of his knowledge and of his emotion. Philosophy is not an emotional theme that may occupy him on occasion. It is his only possible life, his daily response to everything. He lives by thinking, and his one perpetual emotion is that this world, with himself in it, should be the strange world which it is. Everything he thinks or utters will accordingly be an integral part of his philosophy, whether it be called poetry or science or criticism.[6]

Santayana was a poet before he was a philosopher, and his philosophy has retained poetic expression, as well as a preference for sudden insights rather than demonstrated conclusions, for quick flights of fancy rather than the slower pace of reasoning. He disdained all forms of argumentation and any claim to certitude. In his philosophical novel he expressed these sentiments through one of his characters: "The trouble with you philosophers is that you misunderstand your vocation. You ought to be poets, but you insist on laying down the law of the universe, physical and moral, and are vexed with one another because your inspirations are not identical . . . in this novel . . . the views become human persuasions, and the presentation is all the truer for not professing to be true."[7]

Does philosophy, in Santayana's sense of the term, admit of a system: an organic synthesis, with its component parts organized into a logically integrated whole? He frequently

THE MIND OF SANTAYANA

confessed a distrust of any system of philosophy, saying they "are taught only by sects or by individuals setting out to be prophets and to found a sect." Later, however, he had to admit "I now have a system of philosophy," hastily adding "but this system is not intended to found a sect and will never do so. It aspires to be only a contribution to the humanities, the expression of a reflective, selective, and free mind." [8]

Santayana's earlier writings were reflections on diverse topics. Even the five-volume work on the *Life of Reason*, which established him as a philosopher, was loosely reflective: a discursive meditation on the historical phases of man's speculation about the universe. His philosophy at that time was still in a stage of development. His other works during this developmental period were random expressions of opinion through the media of essays, articles, lectures, reviews, poems, and a novel.

Then in 1923 *Scepticism and Animal Faith* appeared, with the frank sub-title: "Introduction to a System of Philosophy." This introductory book was followed in later years by four more volumes collectively titled *Realms of Being*. These five volumes comprise, according to Santayana himself, a systematic presentation of his mature philosophy.

Still expressing a distrust for "the special schools of philosophy, each of which squints and overlooks half the facts and half the difficulties in its eagerness to find in some detail the key to the whole," he insisted that he was merely elaborating upon the obvious experience and common sense of all men. [9] Does this admitted system frankly rest upon a particular metaphysical foundation? Ultimately, or reductively, it must. But Santayana, like so many of his contemporaries, shied away from the label of metaphysics.

My system . . . is *not metaphysical* . . . and I do not disdain being metaphysical because I at all dislike dialectic or disdain

· 58 ·

immaterial things. . . . But logic and mathematics and literary psychology (when frankly literary) are not metaphysical, although their subject matter is immaterial, and their application to existing things is often questionable.[10]

Are the *realms of being,* which enclose Santayana's system of philosophy, comprehensive and exhaustive of reality? He denied such ambitious pretensions: "My system . . . is no *system of the universe.* The Realms of Being, of which I speak, are not parts of a cosmos, nor one great cosmos together; they are only kinds or categories of things which I find conspicuously different and worth distinguishing, at least in my own thoughts. I do not know how many things in the universe at large may fall under each of these classes, or what other Realms of Being may not exist, to which I have no approach or which I have not happened to distinguish in my personal observation of the world." [11]

In *Scepticism and Animal Faith* Santayana establishes a method, discovers essence in intuition, and reduces all knowledge of fact to faith, all definitions and terms to symbols, and all argument to arbitrary dialectic. In the *Realm of Essence* he elaborates his favorite theme: the intuited essence. In the *Realm of Matter* he attempts to defend his cardinal presumption of materialism: dynamic, emergent, and sufficient to sustain a pure naturalism. In the *Realm of Spirit* he develops these basic tenets in the moral sphere. In the *Realm of Truth,* where essence is illustrated in existence, he attempts to fortify his epistemological position and proposes a naturalistic, contemplative life.[12]

I have concentrated upon the notion of essence, as described in these particular volumes, on the recommendation of Santayana himself. Here, he insisted, his mature philosophy is contained and best expressed. All that preceded was a preparation and development; what followed was a consequence and application. In the exposition of Santayana's essentialism, I have attempted not only to define his notion of essence by describing its intrinsic character but also to bring it into clearer focus by showing its extrinsic relations to all that is not essence. This procedure provides a view of the whole structure of Santayana's system of philosophy from the advantageous angle of the keystone of essence.

Essence, of course, is not a fresh concept in philosophy. As a metaphysical constituent of reality, it has been considered by the philosophers of all ages: from the Greeks, through the medieval Schoolmen, to our own contemporaries.

Most recently, Alfred North Whitehead proposed a notion of "eternal object" which bears a marked resemblance to Santayana's notion of essence. Edmund Husserl's "phenomena," as well as his method of arriving at these static appearances, are similar to Santayana's doctrine of intuited essences. René Guenon exposed the "metaphysics" of Indian philosophy in a similar vein. Whitehead's proposition appeared after Santayana published his material on the subject; and Santayana said he was not familiar with either Husserl or Guenon until very late in his life. Hence there is no question of his deriving any influence from them in his own development of the notion of essence.

While essence, the absolute whatness which makes a thing to be what it is, has been the subject of much philosophical speculation, philosophers have varied widely in their interpretation of it. Plato, for example, gave essences an existence apart from things; Santayana gave them no existence at all.

Chapter One

The Discovery of Essence

ACCORDING to Santayana, there is more than one way of discovering essence, as he intends the term in his philosophy. He showed his own preference for an approach through scepticism in the introductory volume to his system of philosophy. But by the time *Realms of Being* appeared, Santayana realized that this rather violent and often complicated approach did not find favor with his readers. "The reconstruction of common sense on that radically sceptical foundation found the reader confused," he said, "and not inclined to recognize and recover his natural reason under the name of animal faith." [1] Consequently he offered other, more direct, routes to the discovery of essence.

One direct passage to essence is through dialectic. Santayana, faithful to his fundamental dichotomy by which the mind is shut off from immediate contact with the universe, describes dialectic as "a construction of ideal forms . . . free from error, because free from any pretence to define ulterior existences." [2] Hence the terms of pure thought, transcending extra-mental objects, are essences. In the construction and interplay of ideal terms, he tells us, "the dialectician, whether his art be called knowledge or not, has discovered the realm of essence (or some province of it) and has devoted himself to exploring it." [3]

A second approach is through aesthetic experience. The sudden impact of beauty can hold fast the attention of the mind and concentrate it to the exclusion of ambient circumstances. The bewitching smile of a child or the first flush of dawn can so fix our mind that we forget all attendant aspects: the squalid garb of the young urchin or the chill and drowsiness in the wake of early morning. The visitor in the art gallery, drawn to the contemplation of a particular picture, may lose all awareness of the passing of time and of other people as he enjoys the harmonious blend of line and color before him. Beauty itself, or any of its particular manifestations, are essences directly apprehended.

Santayana reduces all approaches of the mind to essence to simple attention, a concentration of the mind on whatever logical term or aesthetic appearance arises there. "Awaken attention, intensify it, purify it into white flame, and the actual and unsubstantial object of intuition will stand before you in all its living immediacy and innocent nakedness." [4] You will then have looked upon an essence, stripped of its existential garb and circumstantial ornamentation.

With Santayana, however, we should take the original road through the perilous passage of ultimate scepticism. For at a certain juncture that road bifurcates into the dichotomy that supports the particular doctrine of essence and the general philosophy of Santayana. We must accompany him along that road in order to challenge what he observes along the way. And we must be ready to renounce all previous convictions if we would stay with him through the descending darkness of scepticism. For his endeavor is "to think straight in such terms as are offered to me, to clear my mind of cant and free it from the camp of artificial traditions; but I do not ask anyone to think in my terms if he prefers others." [5]

All the "miasmas of the past, and still more of . . . the present" must be cleared away. For anyone who thinks them "fundamental either in the world or in his own heart . . . can never be a philosopher." After studying the systems of his predecessors, he appeals to those unformulated principles that guided his judgment in understanding their presuppositions and dislodging them. "My system," he says, adding a cautious clause, "if system it can be called, was not so much formed by me as discovered within me . . . my endeavor . . . has been to retreat to the minimum beliefs and radical presuppositions implied in facing a world at all or professing to know anything." [6]

In transcendental criticism, Santayana recognized an apt tool for scepticism. But he realized that Kant and his followers were not critical enough, imposing unwarranted and uncritical assumptions in their assignment of uniform modes of thought to all men. The true sceptic, thoroughly critical, will discard all principles of interpretation in his transcendental flight and then challenge empirical criticism to produce any knowledge of fact whatsoever.

"Criticism," he says, "surprises the soul in the arms of convention." We take so much for granted that the critical investigator may wonder at such an accumulation of unverified opinion; and he will hasten to throw open the doors of doubt to air the cluttered chambers of his stifled soul. How far can the sceptic retreat? Is there a limit, a point of no return? "To be dead," says Santayana, "and have no opinions would certainly not be to discover the truth; but if all opinions are necessarily false, it would at least be not to sin against intellectual honor. Let me then push scepticism as far as I logically can, and endeavor to clear my mind of illusion, even at the price of intellectual suicide." *

Man clings to his conventional beliefs and is not easily persuaded to discard them, even though they may rest upon unquestioned popular opinions. "The philosophy of the com-

* From *Scepticism and Animal Faith*, p. 10. Since the remainder of the quotations used in this chapter are from the same book, reference will be indicated simply by page number in parentheses following.

· 63 ·

mon man," says Santayana, with clever persuasion, "is an old wife that gives him no pleasure, yet he cannot live without her, and resents any aspersions that strangers may cast on her character." (p. 11.) But the sincere sceptic must be ruthless as he thrashes his way to the clearing of his mind. Religion must take the first blow, a rather precipitous one, because it is so "arbitrary" and one "soon learns to discredit established religions." For, as Santayana assures his reader, "mere experience and good sense suggest that all positive religions are false, or at least (which is enough for my present purpose) that they are all fantastic and insecure." (p. 12.) History, especially the kind that proposes a moral interpretation of human events, suffers the same swift fate.

All claims to an external world can be rejected and one can immediately retreat to the datum of consciousness; for, claims Santayana in a sudden transcendental leap, "ideas become beliefs only when by precipitating tendencies to action they persuade me that they are signs of things." (p. 16.) Even the past may be a possible fiction composed by the imagination in the present moment of reflection. But the romantic solipsism of British and German idealists, positing only remembered experience, is inconsistent to the sceptical mind; for even such remembrance evokes physical facts of time and place. "Any solipsism which is not a solipsism of the present moment is logically contemptible." (p. 14.)

Yet the clenched mind, closed to the claim of fact, is pried persistently by one unavoidable pressure, the undeniable pressure of existence with its implication of a relation between subject and object. Is the ego, the self, necessarily implied in the datum of consciousness or intuition? No, because such an analysis "is merely grammatical" since analysis "can never find in the object what, by definition, is all that is found." (p. 22.) Nor should one seize upon factors antecedent to and descriptive of experience, undiscoverable in any momentary actual experience; that is, the double aspect of organ and stimulus, body and environment. The danger here is to confuse the inner nature of experience with its external conditions as natural history reports them and rashly assert that experience is a two-term relationship. By so doing, the fall of a weak sceptic is imminent, for then he will substitute ego for body and illimitable reality for environment and somehow identify the two.

But the sceptic who makes a heroic stand against this assault of beliefs assumed beyond the instant of intuition will accept nothing but the simple, mute appearance given to consciousness. Even change can be denied, because it involves a plurality of elements viewed separately and judged to be connected. The feeling of change is itself an intuition of specious change and not immediately related to actual change. "Actual change," then, "if it is to be known at all, must be known by belief and not by intuition." (p. 26.)

Hence we arrive at a state in which we can discount the cognitive claims of an environment beyond the given scene and of a past and future beyond the specious present. Existence is not given; it is not internal or intrinsic to the theme of intuition. "Existence involves external relations and actual (not merely specious) flux; whereas, however complex a datum may be, with no matter what perspectives opening within it, it must be embraced in a single stroke of apperception, and nothing outside it can belong to it at all." (p. 34.) The datum is simply that which appears; to assert existence of it is to place it in presumptive relations which are not internal to it. I may contemplate a datum without any assertion whatsoever. "Neither its existence nor mine nor that of my belief can be given in any datum." (p. 35.)

The continuous pressure of existence is the strain of life within me, prior to all intuition. I should not confuse *what appears* (which is an ideal object and not an event) with the *event of its appearance*. Existence, then, since it is not included in any datum, is always open to doubt. And so the sceptic can deny all facts and events. He cannot propose his position as a dogma or elaborate it as a doctrine, for in both cases he falls into the traps of event and belief. "Yet," concludes Santayana, "this false dogma that nothing exists is tenable intuitively and, while it prevails, is irrefutable." (p. 40.)

The sceptic, therefore, can rest assured that nothing given exists; for to posit existence even of the datum appearing in intuition is to make a leap of faith. To proclaim the existence of the datum itself or of its intuition is to slide back into the precarious flux of facts and events. This decisive conclusion deserves a full quotation:

> The sceptic turns . . . to the immediate, to the datum; and perhaps for a moment he may fancy he has found true existence there; but if he is a good sceptic he will soon be undeceived. Certainly in the immediate he will find freedom from the struggle of assertion and counter-assertion; no report there, no hypothesis, no ghostly reduplication of the obvious, no ghostly imminence of the notgiven. (Moreover, all that is obvious and self-evident is that which appears; the fact of the appearance is an after-intuition, another appearance.)
>
> Hence an important conclusion which at first seems paradoxical but which reflection will support; namely, that the notion that the datum exists is unmeaning, and if insisted upon is false. That which exists is the fact that the datum is given at that particular moment and crisis in the universe; the intuition, not the datum, is the fact which occurs; and this fact, if known at all, must be asserted at some other moment by an adventurous belief which may be true or false. That which is certain and given, on the contrary, is something of which existence cannot be predicated, and which, until it is used as a description of something else, cannot be either false or true. (pp. 43-45.)

To go beyond the bounds of immediate intuition, to assert anything of the datum, is to rely on animal faith. "Perception is faith; more perception may extend this faith or reform it, but can never recant it except by sophistry." (p. 69.) Knowledge, then, is faith. This is not a new discovery. Indian philosophy recognizes the possible total illusion of existence and proposes a contemplative retreat from the changing scene. Parmenides perceived a possible denial of change, but appealed to dialectic to demonstrate his position, assuming a direct relation between dialectical terms and their objects. Berkeley and Hume made the retreat to intuition, but then erred by identifying ideas with objects of natural knowledge—which are events and facts, not the simple unassertive appearance given in intuition.

Having reached the peak of ultimate scepticism, can the sceptic remain there? What does it profit a sceptic to make such an arduous journey? The workaday world calls him down from his ethereal position at every moment, demanding he descend and be jostled by the crowds in the marketplace. Even if he were left in peace to his inert solitude, what can he accomplish there? He must be mute, drained of existence, of life itself. This is the point of intellectual suicide, the price that can be paid. But to what avail, Santayana asks himself:

> If philosophers wish to abstain from faith, and reduce themselves to intuition of the obvious, they are free to do so, but they will thereby renounce all knowledge. . . . There would be nothing but the realm of essence . . . so that we should be driven back to a nihilism which only silence and death could express consistently; since the least active assertion of it, by existing, would contradict it. (p. 168.)

Santayana admits that "solipsism of the present moment is a violent pose, permitted only to the young philosopher, in his first intellectual despair. . . . A perfect solipsist, therefore, hardly is found amongst men." (pp. 17-18.) Surely scepticism is an impossible way of life. "But," says Santayana, "scepticism is an exercise, not a life; it is a discipline fit to purify the mind of prejudice and render it all the more apt, when the time comes, to believe and to act wisely . . . it is the chastity of the intellect and it is shameful to surrender it too soon or to the first comer." (p. 69.) Yet surrender must be suffered eventually.

A man on the summit of ultimate scepticism, dumb but secure, may choose death as an escape from the doubts below; this solution, however, by no means solves his original problem. Or, as an alternative, he can give up and come down again into the town and share the old conventional uncertainties of the burghers. Yet there is still another alternative. He can contemplate and enjoy the surface appearance of his datum. By so doing he has at least, and at last, seized upon some truth, the self-identity of the theme of intuition. He has discovered the realm of essence, and though he may be forced to leave it momentarily to live and move by animal faith, he can always return to his safe retreat and gaze upon the pure form of a passing essence. Let him seize upon the arrested theme, yet make no claims to it, for himself or for another. Then, says Santayana:

The unintelligible accident of existence will cease to appear to lurk in this manifest being, weighting and crowding it, and threatening it with being swallowed up by nondescript neighbors. It will appear dwelling in its own world, and shining by its own light, however brief may be my glimpse of it; for no date will be written on it, no frame of full or of empty time will shut it in; nothing in it will be addressed to me, nor suggestive of any spectator. It will seem an event in no world, an incident in no experience. The quality of it will have ceased to exist; it will be merely the quality which it inherently, logically, and inalienably is. It will be an ESSENCE. (pp. 73-74.)

The precise nature of essence, the character of its being, will be the subject of the next chapter. For now it is sufficient to recognize the sceptical method Santayana uses in his discovery of essence, as he conceives the term. Scepticism, he says, is pushed beyond the timid stop that Descartes made: "In adopting the method of Descartes, I have sought to carry it further, suspending conventional categories as well as all conventional beliefs." (p. 292.)

The simple contemplation of essences is an attractive vocation to this solitary philosopher who had discovered by experience that the whole world was "ashes in the mouth." If this violent pose of the despairing intellectual could be maintained consistently and permanently, Santayana would choose it. For "a mind enlightened by scepticism and cured of noisy dogma, a mind discounting all reports, and free from all tormenting anxiety about its own fortune or existence, finds in the wilderness of essence a very sweet and marvellous solitude." (p. 76.)

At least in this solitary contemplation of essences, the sceptic is freed from all danger of deception. "If I am content to recognize them for pure essences, they cannot deceive me; they will be like works of literary fiction, more or less coherent, but without any claim to exist on their own account. If I hypostasize an essence into a fact, instinctively placing it in relations which are not given within it, I am putting my trust in animal faith, not in any evidence or implication of my actual experience." (pp. 99-100.) The sceptic can remain within the realm of essence if he so prefers; at any rate, positive experience and certitude are confined to this realm. The realms of nature and of truth are only objects of belief. Intuition becomes illusion if we allow our hypostasizing impulse to take it for anything else, a temptation, Santayana warns, of the natural poet:

In adopting this conclusion of so many great philosophers, that all is illusion, I do so, however, with two qualifications. One is emotional and moral only, in that I do not mourn over this fatality, but on the contrary rather prefer speculation in the realm of essence—if it can be indulged without practical inconvenience—to alleged information about hard facts. It does not seem to me ignominious to be a poet, if nature has made one a poet unexpectedly. . . . The other qualification is more austere: it consists in not allowing exceptions. I cannot admit that some particular essence . . . is the intrinsic essence of all things, so that if I narrow my imagination to that one intuition I shall have intuited the heart and the whole of existence. . . . The life of reason as I conceive it is a mere romance, and the life of nature a mere fable; such pictures have no metaphysical value, even if as sympathetic fictions they had some psychological truth.

The doctrine of essence thus renders my scepticism invincible and complete, while reconciling me with it emotionally. (pp. 100-101.)

If scepticism is "an exercise, not a life," neither is the mute meditation of an essence a way of life. Life involves action, events, memory and expectation. If there is no certainty beyond the self-evidence of an essence, then living is a necessary pledge of faith: "animal faith," for it is a kind of instinctive "open-mouthedness" proper to, and presumed in, animal life. The admission that nothing given exists is not incompatible with belief in things not given. Now the good sceptic should consider "what objects animal faith requires me to posit and in what order; without for a moment forgetting that my assurance of their existence is only instinctive, and my description of their nature only symbolic." (p. 106.)

The sense of duration of an essence, held in intuition, suggests an element of time, not as attributed to the essence itself, which is eternal, but to its grasp in intuition. The reappearance of an essence, by which we attribute sameness to an object, indicates the character of identity. Both of these primary observations are hazardous excursions into animal faith, but in the order of evidence they rank first—not nec-

essarily as true postulates, but as convenient and suitable beliefs. Then demonstration, or dialectic, can be employed on
the assumption that I can relate terms of discourse, of themselves simple and inert essences. Says Santayana:

> The validity of demonstration is accordingly a matter of faith
> only, depending on the assumption of matters of fact inca-
> pable of demonstration. I must believe that I noted the terms
> of the argument separately and successively if I am to assert
> anything in identifying them or pronouncing them equivalent,
> or if the conclusion in which they appear now is to be rele-
> vant in any way to the premises in which they appeared orig-
> inally. (p. 118.)

Santayana, the good and true sceptic, must come down from
the summit of ultimate scepticism if he intends to talk at all.
For in order to say anything *about* essence, or anything else
for the matter (including the discovery of essence in the first
place)—then he must admit the validity of discourse, at least,
as he would put it, as a "primary belief." "If I confine myself
to the given essence without admitting discourse about it, I
exclude all analysis of that essence, or even examination of it.
I must simply stare at it, in a blank and timeless aesthetic
trance." (p. 119.)

After accepting discourse as the only possible means of
proceeding, the sceptic is no longer purely such; he is ready
to submit his virginal scepticism to the brutal fact of existence. Which particular existent shall be admitted first into
the purified chambers of the sceptical mind?

Essences appear and disappear, and "if I consider what they
are, and how they appear, I see that this appearance is an accident to them; that the principle of it is a contribution from
my side, which I call intuition. The difference between essence and intuition . . . seems to me profound and certain.
They belong to two different realms of being. The first existence, then, of which a sceptic who finds himself in the

presence of random essences may gather reasonable proof, is the existence of the intuition to which those essences are manifest." (p. 133.)

So far, existence is predicated only of a power of intuition that presumes to discourse about essences. Reality is still only internal. Then I note the unmistakable sense of *shock*, interrupting discourse and directing intent, implying that something *happens*—and, moreover, happens to *me*. This I call *experience*. "In brute experience, or shock, I have not only a clear indication, for my ulterior reflection, that I exist, but a most imperious summons at that very moment to *believe* in my existence." (p. 141.) And if the sense of shock does not deceive me, then there must have been a passage from the state of pre-shock to post-shock. Perceiving this experience as a whole I discover "a wonderful and ambiguous presence of the absent and persistence of the receding, which is called *memory*." (p. 141.) Santayana thus emerges from the momentary solipsism and reaches outside of intuition:

> Experience of shock, if not utterly delusive, accordingly, establishes the validity of memory and of transitive knowledge. It establishes realism. If it be true that I have ever had any experience, I must not only have existed unawares in order to gather it, but I am justified in explicitly asserting a whole realm of existence, in which one event may contain realistic knowledge of another. . . . Belief in experience is belief in nature, however vaguely nature may as yet be conceived. . . . (p. 142.)

Santayana must, and does, admit that even this sense of shock and all that it implies could be no more than an essence. But it is time to escape the dead end of intuition and reach into other realms. The simple apprehension of essence, stripped of existential relations, is a blind alley completely walled up. The sceptic must leap over that wall, boosted by animal faith, into the existent. Otherwise, he admits, "I should be condemned forever to blank watching and sheer wonder." He descends from his summit reluctantly, and lest we minimize such a feat he bravely declares: "This is so great a step that most minds cannot take it." (p. 144.)

With Santayana we have approached essence through scepticism. It is the path he prefers, and along which he sets up definite postulates which support his whole philosophy. At the summit of ultimate scepticism, in the "solipsism of the present moment," we have viewed the simple datum of intuition, shelled of all existential content. *We have discovered essence.* The descent from that breathless summit was necessary in order to posit a discursive self and a stimulating universe to provide the fodder for further speculation. It was an interesting excursion, going up and coming back. And along the way we noted the observations the philosopher made. We shall come back to them later on.

The task remains to delineate the notion of essence more clearly, both by scrutinizing its absolute character and its relative significance with regard to other notions.

Chapter Two

Essence Defined

SANTAYANA'S notion of essence made its formal philosophical debut in *Essays in Critical Realism*, published in 1920. He had, however, occasionally mentioned this notion in articles which appeared prior to that year.[1] But it was in this collaborative work of criticism, particularly through his contribution, "Three Proofs of Realism," that the notion gained formal recognition as a critical postulate towards solving the epistemological problem.

This notion of essence was accepted by most of his collaborators (enthusiastically by some, grudgingly by others) as the mediating term in their re-presentative theory of knowledge. In that volume, which counter-attacked the earlier Neo-Realism, Drake understood the notion of essence as "characters and character complexes." (p. 22.) Pratt called essences "logical universals, while things are spatial or at least temporal . . . the two cannot be identified." (p. 102.) Rogers described essence as the character "assigned to some reality existing independently of the knowledge process." (p. 117.) Strong more succinctly summed up the notion as "the logical essence of the real thing . . . its *what* divorced from its *that*." (p. 223.) Santayana, in this first formal presentation of the notion, said that the "object of pure sense or pure thought, with no belief super-added, an object inwardly complete and individual, but without external relations or physical status, is what I call an essence." (p. 168.)

In his five-volume synthesis, Santayana described essence in various terms and phrases: *all possible terms in mental discourse, ideal terms at the command of fancy, nameless phantoms of feeling and intuition, every specious object actually present to intuition, some sensuous or logical term, datum, appearance, image, feeling, being, form, form of being, description, an ideal theme.* Specifically he employed the term essence to describe such items as *color, pain, beauty, blue, sound, sky-blue, the form of a hollow sphere, B-flat,* and *nausea.*

In the previous chapter some significance of the term was gained by a pursuit of doubt to its farthest reach. From the summit of ultimate scepticism we have viewed the infinite vista of the realm of essence. Santayana offers vivid descriptions of his oft-contemplated realm.

> The realm of essence . . . is simply the unwritten catalogue, prosaic and infinite, of all the characters possessed by such things as happen to exist, together with the characters which all different things would possess if they existed. It is the sum of mentionable objects, of terms about which or in which, something might be said.[2]

The final sentence quoted above is important, because it definitely states that this notion applies equally to that which is given in intuition and the descriptive term employed in discourse about it. *Terms about which or in which* includes, therefore, the verbal or mental term and the object signified by that term.

Elsewhere he speaks of the realm of essence as "an infinite Koran—or the Logos that was in the beginning—written in invisible but indelible ink, prophesying all that Being could ever be or contain. . . ."[3] The sceptic's approach to this realm, as we have seen, is to arrest the datum of consciousness and strip it of all adventitious aspects, all assertions or denials. By so penetrating to the core of the datum, the ghostly and unsubstantial inhabitant of the realm of essence appears. "Nothing will remain but some appearance now; and that which appears, when all gratuitous implication of a world beyond or of a self here are discarded, will be an *essence*." [4] He develops the notion of essence as an appearance:

> It is an appearance only in the sense that its nature is wholly manifest, that it is a specific being, which may be mentioned, thought of, seen, or defined, if any one has the wit to do so. But its own nature says nothing of any hidden circumstances that shall bring it to light, or any adventitious mind that shall discover it. It lies simply in its own category. If a color, it is just this color; if a pain, just this pain. Its appearance is not an event; its presence is not an experience; for there is no surrounding world in which it can arise, and no watchful spirit to appropriate it. The sceptic has here withdrawn into the intuition of a surface form, without roots, without origin or environment, without a seat or a locus; a little universe, an immaterial absolute theme, rejoicing merely in its own quality. This theme, being out of all adventitious relations and not in the least threatened with not being the theme it is, has not the contingency nor the fortunes proper to an existence; it is simply that which it inherently, logically, and unchangeably is. [5]

Having viewed the emergence of essence through ultimate scepticism and having examined the notion in varying contexts, we can attempt to define it more precisely. We can do that, first of all, by indicating the particular properties or attributes of essence: what it is positively and how it is distinguished from other notions with which it might be confused.

The principle of essence, Santayana tells us, is *identity*. The being of each essence is entirely exhausted by its definition, not its verbal description but that definite character which distinguishes one essence from every other essence. Here Santayana employs a Scholastic principle, not as distinguishing being from nothing but as distinguishing one essence from every other essence. He says of essences:

> They are what they are; and of all the meanings of the word *is*—existence, substance, equivalence, definition, etc.—the most radical and proper is that in which I may say of anything that it is what it is. This observation does not commit me to any classification of the object or to any assertion of its existence. I merely note its idiosyncrasy, its qualitative identity, which enables me to distinguish it, study it, and hold it fast in my intent, so that I may eventually frame a definition of it, and perhaps assert or deny its existence.[6]

This self-identity of each essence, distinguishing it from every other essence, possible or actual, renders an essence *individual*. Hence in the realm of essence there can be no question of mistaken identity or self-contradiction. These difficulties arise with respect to natural existences or meanings conferred; but in themselves all alternatives are genuine essences and the groping mind (in an instance of verbal contradiction) merely hesitates between essences.

Yet this very inalienable individuality of each essence renders it a universal as well; "for being perfectly self-contained and real only by virtue of its intrinsic character, it contains no reference to any setting in space or time, and stands in no adventitious relations to anything. Therefore without forfeiting its absolute identity it may be repeated or reviewed any number of times." [7]

Santayana insists upon "the universal and the individual being so far from contrary that they are identical." [8] Hence in the intuition of essence we find "an ideal individual which being individuated only by its intrinsic quality, not by any external or dynamic relations (since none are given), is also a universal."⁹ Thus universality is predicated of essence because it is an ideal term, devoid of any material or adventitious aspects, unrealized in the external context of time and place.¹⁰

Essences are also *infinite*, since of themselves they are nonexistent and therefore unlimited and undetermined by any extrinsic connotation. Simply because some essence has not been exemplified in nature or has never appeared to anyone's intuition are not sufficient reasons for denying its being. "To deny the being of essence, because it may happen to be unrealized, is self-contradictory: for if it is not realized, it must have a quality, distinguishing it from realized forms."¹¹ Paradoxically, then, to deny an essence is to admit it!

Essences cannot be exhausted by any intuition of them, for even granting such a comprehensive intuition the very event of that intuition and its peculiar extraordinariness would be essences. It is the note of identity, that unique character of every essence, which assures an infinite realm of essence. Santayana continues on this note:

> In one sense, indeed, the being of any essence implies that of every other; for if any one essence is assured of its being because it is a distinguishable something, obviously every other distinguishable something is assured of its being on the same ground; so that an infinite multitude of essences is implied, if you will, in the being of any essence.¹²

A last positive property of essence is that of *eternity;* all essences are eternal. Santayana intends eternity in a proper sense: not as an interminable extension of time in the existential order, but that changeless quality which places a being altogether outside of time. For essences do not exist, except by a possible transitory embodiment in existence. Of themselves, they are extra-temporal, and any sense of endurance in the intuition of them is a temporal aspect of the event of intuition, not of the essence intuited. Of the eternity of essences, Santayana says:

> Eternity, taken intrinsically, has nothing to do with time, but is a form of being which time cannot usher in or destroy. . . . But intuition peruses eternal being in time; consequently, so long as I am attending to an essence, this essence seems to me to *endure;* and when, after an interval, I revert to it or any feature of it, this feature seems to me *to be identical* with what it was. This identity and this duration are not properly predicated of essence in its own realm.[13]

The pure notion of essence must not be confused with other notions in which "there is some ambiguity, some reference to contingent existence, which limits their scope, and renders them altogether confusing if taken as synonyms for essential being."[14] The following exclusions are noted:

Essence is not possible being. The notion of possibility and impossibility, says Santayana, has no application to the realm of essence but to the field of discourse, where one intends to consider one essence to the exclusion of another under the same name. Nothing contradicts itself, except in the limited mind in which determined discourse may blur the inherent distinctness of different essences. How can anything preclude being thought of if a mind arose capable of conceiving it? "The meaning," he says, "can only be that my own imagination, in some particular instance, has got into a tangle, and that in speaking of the round square or the son of a barren woman I have lost the meaning of my terms; and what I call impossibility is only the suspense of my thought between two possibilities."[15]

Essences are not images. An image, although an unsubstantial appearance, is selected. Furthermore, it is a reproduction or replica of the actual, of particular human sensations. Images participate in this actuality since the imagination of them occurs at definite times and places. Images, therefore, cannot be identified with essences which are inert, originals rather than replicas, and eternal: beyond the confines of time and the actuality of sense. *Essences are not forms.* Forms may manifest essences but are not identified with them.[16] The precise distinction Santayana makes between essence and form, since he uses the words interchangeably, is not at all clear. His principal objection to their identification seems to be based upon his rejection of Platonic idealism in so far as it attributed a subsistent ontological status to universal ideas and assigned some regnant and operational power to them.[17] Accepting form in the sense of the Platonic εἶδος, the distinction between this notion and Santayana's notion of essence is apparent. But the Aristotelian notion of form, either substantial or accidental, is not considered here, at least explicitly.

Essences are not abstractions. They are immaterial but not necessarily abstracted from matter. They are not abstractions in the sense of a psychological operation; this is obvious. But are they the terms or products of that cognitional process? Occasionally, Santayana admits, and then only in a temporal sense. One sees an apple, for example, and this object may in turn "suggest" a sphere. In this instance, roundness for this particular person comes as "a late idea" and so "for that person the sphere will be something abstract, not indeed in its essence, but in its mode of reaching manifestation: an act of abstraction happens first to have revealed this essence to this man." [18] But Santayana does not want to be caught in an admission of abstraction, which implies a direct and realistic process of knowledge. Ideas are only signals, he insists, and man can directly intuit roundness without previously considering a round object.[19] Only the possibility of repeating an essence under different adventitious aspects makes essences "seem abstract or general, when in reality they are the only individuals." [20]

ESSENCE DEFINED

Essences are not sensations or thoughts. Sensation and intellection are events; they are always fresh events even when
turned upon the same object. They proceed, as operational
events, part after part, and so belong to the existential order. Essences, however, are inert and simple. But is the idea,
the cognitional term, an essence? It is important to note that
Santayana answers this question negatively. He gives the example of the idea of God: "If I think of God, the essence
before me, my passing notion of the divine nature, individ-
uates that thought of mine, and makes it possible for discourse afterward to attribute it to me; but my thought was
not God as it conceived God. . . ." [21] An essence, he insists, may be conceived by an idea but is not to be confused
with the idea or identified with it. It is an idea "only in the
Platonic or graphic sense of being a theme open to consideration." [22]

Essences are not intrinsic, constituitive qualities of things.
Santayana strongly inveighs against those who are snared into
the "hypostasis of given essences" by attributing an essence
intuited to the object intended. The sphere of action must
be distinguished from the language in which experience is expressed. Pain, for example, should not be ascribed to the particular bodily member in which perception projects the feeling.[23] To emphasize his point, the philosopher gives an example of a man looking at the sky. The blueness and roundness of the sky are not intrinsic or constitutive parts of the
sky, nor should these essences be localized in the nerves or
the brain. They are qualities of the sky only relatively, relative to the observer who happens to observe them.[24] Things
are not what they seem, nor do they exist in the very terms
in which they appear. Appearance and reality must not be
confused, for we do not directly intuit things. "Intuition of
things," he says, "is a contradiction in terms." [25]

OTHER ASPECTS OF ESSENCE

Pure Being falls under Santayana's consideration, either as an essence taken separately, or as a background or substrate to all essences. He explains: "Pure Being supplies, as it were, the logical or aesthetic matter which all essences have in common, and which reduces them to comparable modes on one plane of reality. Pure Being is thus found in all essences somewhat as light is in all colors or life in all feeling." [26] Pure Being, then, is understood in this omnipresent and basic sense. All essences are pure in their precise, definitive character; but pure Being is present in all of them "as space is in all geometric forms." Furthermore, pure Being is not to be confused with existence: the latter is experienced as a "dull strain"; the former arises from a "clear, sharp intuition." Nor are they necessarily connected; one can directly intuit pure Being without a previous process of abstraction. In fact, "in order to reach the intuition of pure Being, it is requisite to rise altogether above the sense of existence." [27] Far from identifying being and essence, he warns, we must recognize their opposition. "Existence exists by virtue of oppositions in the place, time, and exclusive characters of particulars: being has being by virtue of its universal identity. This is true of the being of each individual essence; and it is true preeminently of pure Being." [28]

Non-Being, on the other hand, signifies a privation of essence; nothing means "nothing of that sort." This element of privation pertains to every essence, since each essence being itself necessarily denies every other essence. Hence, by what we would call the transcendental unity of being, "all essences . . . partake of non-being, and pure Being does so in an eminent degree since it excludes the special forms of being proper to all others." [29]

The word "simple" has been used to describe essence; but strictly speaking it should be applied to the intuition of essence rather than essence itself. For essences, Santayana tells us, may be either simple or complex: depending on whether they are given in their entirety or are considered partially. A landscape is an essence, but so are all the elements that compose it. Whether the whole, or a single part, is attended to, each is itself, maintaining an intrinsic unity. "There is no limit to this complexity in unity: the system of any world is one essence; the whole realm of essence is one essence." [30]

Since any essence is an eternal form of being, without reference to any other, "no essence . . . can imply any other in the sense of excluding from the realm of essence the opposite of the essence implied, or any different complement." [31] Santayana explains:

> From itself an essence may exclude anything; in fact it excludes everything not itself, but when a thing or a thought is said to preclude another, this happens only by virtue of adventitious laws of nature.[32]

Color, for example, is revealed simultaneously with extension, but is not therefore inseparable from it or from the object believed to exist in three dimensions. Of itself color is "a most pungent and positive essence, which can come and go while extension remains the same; and it is only an accident of human sensibility that no organ yields something which might be called color without extension. . . ." [33]

Essences, it should be remembered, can be embodied in matter or simply given in intuition.[34] Events, too, have their essences and are universals which may or may not occur as historical truths. But to these eventual essences, Santayana gives a special name—*tropes*, referring to the essence of a sequence of moments in an event under the form of eternity. The essence of an event is distinguished from the event itself in that the event exemplifies the trope in being enacted.[35] They can be "imagined, felt, conceived, contemplated, or somehow directly revealed to spirit." [36] Whether simple or complex, they are all primary: in themselves utterly simple, one, individual. For examples of this simplicity, even in complex essences, Santayana mentions:

1. *the feeling of pity*, discounting the occasion or object, the historical or emotional conditionings of the feeling.

2. *the perception of distance*, in itself and devoid of the specious essences which may help to describe its genesis and component setting, whether objective or subjective.

3. *the sense of beauty*, as a simple and sudden reactive feeling, regardless of its objective occasion.[37]

Finally, I would like to add a paragraph from a personal letter received from Santayana in which he sums up this notion of essence:

The first motto facing p. 1 of my *Realm of Essence* gives you the definition that Plato gave for that category of being: *that which never changes*. This is chosen by contrast with Heraclitus's "all things flow." "Essence" or "idea" is therefore not a "thing" or "existence" at all, but a definable character. If Mrs. Smith and Mrs. Jones have twins, the two pairs will be different from each other, and, from moment to moment, different from themselves: but the essence of "twins," as the dictionary defines it, will be identical in both.[38]

Conclusion

These various descriptions, supplied by Santayana, help us to view his notion of essence from different angles and offer us different aspects. A single precise definition is not available. The philosopher never gives one, and his various statements of the meaning of essence involve differing connotations. The concept is too simple to admit of essential definition, since we are speaking of essence itself, without a constitution of either physical or metaphysical parts. Yet, paradoxically, Santayana's concept of essence seems too complex: a composite, an admixture of metaphysical and physical realities. The most that can be hoped for is a descriptive definition, either intrinsically through a notation of its properties and accidents; or extrinsically through an indication of its origin and purpose.

Difficulties abound. For example, Santayana tells us that "nothing given is either physical or mental, in the sense of being intrinsically a thing or a thought; it is just a quality of being." [39] Yet, he says that "a datum is by definition a theme of attention, a term in passing thought." [40] But a "term of passing thought" seems to be an idea, and we get this impression from other passages as well; yet he has warned us that essences are not ideas. Nor is an essence the object of thought, since "intuition of things is a contradiction." He speaks of essences as "terms in mental discourse," yet they are not words; for we are not to confuse essences with their verbal descriptions. All of these difficulties will be considered again in the critical section of this work. It is enough for the present to indicate the difficulties of defining the intrinsic character of Santayana's notion of essence.

It may help to consider, briefly, the extrinsic causal quality of this essence: its beginning and end, origin and use. We would need a detailed study of Santayana's notion of man and how he operates in the universe. For now, at least, we can glimpse the origin of essence as it arises in intuition. This is a purely transcendental mode of cognition, altogether internal. Essences are not abstracted from existents; they are not plucked from external objects. They simply arise in intuition.

What is intuition? The philosopher calls it "an act of attention occurring here and now." [41] Or again: "the light of awareness lending actuality to some essence." [42] Hence, by intuition, Santayana intends an immediate apprehension or awareness, consciousness in act. "The organ of intuition," he says, "is an animal psyche, governed by the laws of material life, in other words, by habit. . . ." [43] He explains these relations between psyche and intuition more fully:

> Intuition would be impossible without an underlying animal life, a psyche; for how should the sheer light of intuition actualise itself, or choose the essence on which it should fall. A psyche, the hereditary organization and movement of life in an animal, must first exist and sustain itself by its "intelligent" adaptations to the ambient world: but these adaptations are not conscious until, by virtue of their existence, intuition arises; and intuition arises when the inner life of the animal, or its contact with external things, is expressed in some actual appearance, in some essence given in feeling or thought. The psyche and the material circumstances, by their special character and movement, determine the choice and succession of themes on which intuition shall be employed in some particular person; in so far as spirit is kindled there at all, it will have raised those themes to the plane of essence. [44]

Essences, then, somehow arise in intuition by "the special character and movement" of both the psyche and the material circumstances. Santayana is fond of pictorially describing the psyche immersed in the matter of man, from which it somehow emerged to surface life. Spirit is active, and by intuition lights up an essence awakening the vegetative psyche to consciousness of *this* new element. Whatever *this* is —a perception, a feeling, a term—is an essence. The purpose, or final cause, of essence is, therefore, its functional awareness that enables man to think or speak or be at all; for an essence becomes a sign or symbol of whatever is experienced or encountered in action. [45]

The "incarnated" essences, ephemerally caught up in the irrational flux of matter, may cause the rise of essence in intuition. But apparently these two essences are not separate or distinct qualities; but the one quality or essence which happens to be both in a thing and given in intuition. The problematic relation between the two refers to the cognitional aspect of essence, to be treated in another chapter. The important note in either instance of essence is its intrinsic and, for Santayana, absorbing *thisness*.

Therefore, I would venture, in my own terms, a definition of Santayana's notion of essence: *the quiddity of any being whatsoever*. We can elaborate that definition by adding: *without reference to any status: possible or actual, ontological or logical, physical or ideal, conceptual or eventual, simple or complex*.

Chapter Three

Essence and Existence

SANTAYANA claims that he distinguishes essence from existence; and, contrary to the opinion of Royce, he insists he does not separate the two.[1] While he justifies this position of non-separation on the basis of a belief in actualized essences in existents, yet he opposes these two realities vehemently. The extent of that opposition, the relation of essence to existence, and the nature of existence itself must be examined.

BELIEF IN EXISTENCE

The tight grasp on essence, held in the solipsism of the present moment, is released in the consequent moment that admits existence. Existence, implying external relations, can never be given in intuition; it is an object of belief. "I shall attribute existence," says the philosopher, "to a flux of natural events which can never be data of intuition, but only objects of a belief which men and animals, caught in that flux themselves, hazard instinctively." [2] An instinctive tension propels the animal into such belief, indeed requires it in the active vicissitudes of life. But to hazard this belief one must break away from the security of intuition. Santayana explains:

[Intuition] cannot break through into existence unless it loses itself and submits to transition; and the foretaste or aftertaste of such transition, present in feeling, must posit something eventual, something absent from intuition, if even the sense or idea of existence is to arise at all. Then the mind engaged in action may begin to live by faith in the outlying conditions of life, and by an instinctive tension towards obscure events.[3]

This primary belief, although instinctive and practically necessary, is nevertheless an unreasonable pledge of faith and a precarious plunge into the unknown. Intuition is safe and certain. What it beholds it beholds. But the transition to existence places one in a perilous passage. "The measure of confidence," Santayana admits, "with which I have spoken of essence forsakes me when I approach existence." Faced with the prospect of reaching out to a fluctuating ambient world and assuming that his experience of it is similar to that of others—monstrous assumptions which he says can "never be justified"—the philosopher dolefully confesses: "I am at a loss." [4] He then proceeds to describe that inaccessible natural world in a volume of more than two hundred pages.

The approach to existence from transcendental reflection is, he admits, one's own dogmatism "by which objects of belief are defined and marshaled, of such a character and in such order as intelligent action demands." [5] He then marshals his definitions and propositions in the order in which he perceives them.

SUBSTANCE THE PRINCIPLE OF EXISTENCE

Essences come and go in intuition; we presume, then, that things change. Hence "something, not essence . . . actualizes and limits the manifestation of every essence that figures in nature or appears before the mind. To this dark principle of existence we give the name of substance. . . ." [6] Faith in substance, being only an implication of action (that which is encountered in action) is "the most irrational, animal, and primitive of beliefs." [7] Substance, the dark principle of existence, is obscure to the light of transcendental spirit. "To pure spirit," he says, "substance and all its ways must remain always dark, alien and impertinent. . . . What ghostly thing, it says to itself, is this Speaker behind the voice, this Meaning behind the vision, this dark substance behind the fair appearance?" [8]

Although substance is "dark" and "alien," Santayana sees it well enough to provide a detailed description of its nature and functions. To begin with, he warns us that the substance of which he speaks "is not metaphysical but physical substance . . . the varied stuff of the world which I meet in action . . . simply whatever the physical substance may be which is found in things or between them." [9] Substance cannot explain things, since they are its parts. "If substance were some metaphysical principle . . . it might be expected to 'explain' existence as a whole; but it ought not then to be called a substance." [10]

MATTER IS THE ONLY SUBSTANCE

When Santayana comes to describe substance he immediately implies his presumption of materialism. He describes properties of substance which could apply only to material substances and then concludes to the principle with which he began in the first place. After ascribing these material conditions to substance—some of them "indispensable" properties, others "presumable"—he draws the obvious inference: "a substance possessing these functions and these characteristics has a familiar name: it is called matter." [11] Substance and matter, then, are interchangeable as terms. *Substance is matter.*

According to Santayana's own restricted notion of sub-

stance—a basic tenet and cardinal principle of his whole philosophy—the notion of "spiritual substance" is "a self-contradictory notion at bottom." Why? Because, as he tells us,
completing the circle, "substance is a material and spirit is
an entelechy, or perfection of function realized. . . ." [12]
What is matter? Here again we see things in a transcendental glass, darkly. We cannot know the precise constitution of matter. For the order of nature is something that
happens and is not conceived, "so that no sensuous or graphic
or mathematical transcript of it should be so pressed as to
be substituted for it." [13] Santayana may not press his own
transcript of nature, but he offers it with the assurance of
presenting the original copy.

Matter, since it is equated with substance, is likewise "the
principle of existence." [14] It is "all things in their potentiality, and therefore the condition of all their excellence or
possible perfection." [15] Matter is not static or inert. Rather,
it is dynamic and self-subsisting, requiring no motion or organization from without. It is "the substance of our world,
and the principle of life and death in it." [16] The realm of
matter is the field of action. Since our own action and existence are interpolated into a world already existing, *therefore:* "our existence and purposes . . . were evidently drawn
from that very world on which they react. From the point
of view of origins, therefore, the realm of matter is the matrix and the source of everything: it is nature, the sphere of
genesis, the universal mother." [17]

Santayana admits that "the dominance of matter in every
existing being, even when that being is spiritual, is the great
axiom of materialism, to which this whole book [*Realm of
Matter*] is only a corollary." [18] A hard saying! But he immediately offers to "take away half its inhuman sting." This
amelioration is accomplished by inviting us to recognize mat-

ter not as something crass and inferior to us but as our creator. "Matter is a primeval plastic substance of unknown potentiality, perpetually taking on new forms. The gist of materialism is that these forms are all passive and precarious,
while the plastic stress of matter is alone creative and, as far
as we can surmise, indestructible." [19] Matter, it would seem,
determines itself. It is potential—"the existing potentiality of
specific things" [20]—yet actualizing as a creative agent producing its own forms.

ESSENCE IN RELATION TO EXISTENCE AND SUBSTANCE

Essences are the "forms of substance." [21] They make things
to be what they are, for "everything that exists is confined
to a specific character at a particular time and place; if it
escaped from those bonds it would cease to be itself." [22]
They make physical change possible and, as given in intuition, enable the mind to describe this change.[23] There is no
question here of two essences in the sense of two distinct
entities, not merely distinct but separate—the one a form spe-
cifying a substance and the other a logical counterpart in
intuition—which are somehow identified or even contrasted
to terminate in knowledge of fact. There is one essence
which may be exemplified in nature or given in intuition.[24]
In a natural substance an essence is "embodied" or "incarnated;" yet we have been warned not to identify essence
with the substance it specifies nor consider it a constitutive
part of that substance. And since the essence given in intuition is not a "true description" of the substance encountered in action, we must have two different essences involved
in cognition. But this observation belongs to the following
chapter where the role of essence in cognition will be discussed.

Since essence specifies a particular substance, any change

in that substance, total or partial, demands a change of essence. According to Santayana, "Any substance differs from the essence of that substance, and any event from the essence of that event, in that it can arise and perish . . . externally, by intruding into a field of irrelevant entities, or quitting that field; and then again internally, by changing the order of its parts, each of which, in a thing or an event, has an individuality internal to it, and is a concrete component, not merely a fragment or aspect of the whole." [25]
When essence is exemplified by a fact it simply acquires external relations. He explains:

> It is only by such embodiment in matter that essences can be loosened, as it were, from their essential setting and turned into the characters of facts; or rather—since their essential setting is eternal and holds them even while embodiments of them are passing through existence—it is only by being distributed in the field of action that essences can add for a moment external and variable relations to those which their proper nature involves.[26]

The contemplative philosopher often complains of the brutal assault on essence by existence, even calling it the "rape" of pure essence. Yet the embodiment of an essence in nature does not, it seems, violate the eternal character of that essence. The constant flux of existence enables the ethereal essence to elude the grasp of its captor, except to permit momentary "external relations." This would seem to imply more than merely a "distinction" between essence and existence. For example:

> Existence itself is a surd, external to the essence which it may illustrate and irrelevant to it; for it drags that essence into some here and now, or some then and there; and the things so created, far from being identical with their essence at any moment, exist by eluding it, encrusting it in changing relations, and continually adopting a different essence; so that

nothing accurate can be said of a thing supposed to bridge two moments of time.[27]

When an essence is caught in the flux of existence and incorporated in a substance, it acquires a frame of external relations, but it is not identified with the substance which is "more and other than the essence." For, says Santayana, "at each point substance must exemplify some essence, of which, then and there it creates an instance; but it does so by setting that essence in a frame of external relations; so that substance is always more and other than the essence which it exemplifies at any point." [28]

Existence, Santayana insists, is irrational and "chaotic." The whole world of fact and fortune is utterly unintelligible and in itself accidental. He says:

> Existence is indeed distinguishable from the platonic essences that are embodied in it precisely by being a conjunction of things mutually irrelevant, a chapter of accidents, a medley improvised here and now for no reason, to the exclusion of myriad other farces which, so far as their ideal structure is concerned, might have been performed just as well. This world is contingency and absurdity incarnate, the oddest of possibilities masquerading momentarily as a fact.[29]

Such a chaotic universe can provide no explanation of itself; existence is dumb as to its origin or goal. "Existence (as the least insight into essence shows) is necessarily irrational and inexplicable. It cannot, therefore, contain any principle of explanation *a priori*. . . ." [30] How then does this blind and dumb existence happen to embody or exemplify selected essences in particular forms and patterns? Does the essence choose the substance to which it will succumb? No, for "this descent or incarnation of essences cannot be their own doing, since all essences are inert and nonexistent." [31] Does an extrinsic creative power confer forms? By no means. Then how? Oddly enough it is matter, the principle of irrational existence, that performs this marvelous feat. How? It just happens:

> Even the thinnest creations of spirit . . . are products of the realm of matter and possible only within it. Incarnation is no voluntary emanation from above; it is a dire event, a budding torment, here below. A world of accidents, arbitrary and treacherous, first lends to the eternal a temporal existence and a place in the flux.[32]

A "budding torment" explains the universe, its order of forms and functions.

COROLLARIES

Following the "great axiom of materialism" to its logical consequences, what follows? Is there any order in the universe, and if so how explain it? Are there any natural laws? Is there any causality? How does spirit, the immaterial, arise from the material? What is man: that strange conjunction of the material and immaterial? Let Santayana answer these questions briefly.

In discussing nature, Santayana relies on the vague notions of "forward tensions" and "lateral tensions." There are "relations" and "tropes;" and the picturesque terms "pictorial space" and "sentimental time" are the ideal essences corresponding to physical space and duration. All matter is in flux, exhibiting a constant forward tension (which in man is called *will*). Fortunately for us, the irrational flux "for the time being has been somewhat canalized in our parts of the universe, and the lateral tensions are partly held in check, and turned to sustenance, for the benefit of some persisting organisms. . . ."[33] Potentialities which develop into intricate actualities, at once functional and beautiful, are not intrinsic or the realization of a predestined essence, but simply a wonderful result of a proper juxtaposition of external relations and cosmic tensions.[34]

What of the apparent order manifested in nature with its implication of necessary laws? Santayana admits that such natural regularity is "prevalent," yet denies a rational origin or end to nature. "Necessity, in nature," he says, "is only an irrational propulsion which, as a matter of fact, is prevalent." [35] Necessity, he assures us, is accidental! "In a contingent world necessity is a conspiracy of accidents" and "this precipitation of accidents is the work of matter, shifting its equilibrium and modifying its strains." [36] All change, in fact, is due to this shifting of equilibrium.[37]

Not only is the necessary accidental, but, by another curious turnabout, what is ordinary is extraordinary; for "the actual order of nature . . . is . . . most miraculous when most regular." [38]

Dynamic matter manifests certain repeated modes of action with considerable regularity. These he calls *tropes*, in the sense of habitual directions or procedures in the behavior of matter. These tropes are mechanical because they are repeated with regularity, vital because they are spontaneous, and they arise from the dynamic tensions of matter. Tropes should not be called laws, even when law is understood as "merely a formula or an average, or an equation probably approximatively realized in a certain plane of events." [39] The danger is that this notion of law is too often raised to the stature of an idol, a metaphysical power compelling events to obey it. Santayana offers to explain the reality of law. Having given us the primary axiom of materialism, he now adds two complementary axioms:

> I think that the reality of law can be briefly expressed in two maxims: one, that whatsoever happens anywhere, happens there spontaneously, as if it had never occurred before and would never occur again; the other, that whatsoever spon-

taneously happens once will have spontaneously happened before and will spontaneously happen again, wherever similar
elements are in the same relations.[40]

In other words, to be a devout materialist one must also
call regularity spontaneity. The disciple of Matter must hold
fast to his faith in the basic axiom of his creed, despite any
evidence to the contrary. Even the supernatural must become
a naturalized citizen in the realm of matter. "The supernatural
is nothing but an extension of the natural into the unknown. . . ." [41] What appears to be "miraculous" is only an
unexpected turn of nature, whose ways are not our ways and
cannot be determined or accurately measured by us.[42] To set
limits on nature's activities is sheer egotism, or rash assumption hustled into the service of private interests.

Repetition and regularity in nature cannot be conceived
as manifestations of fixed law. The concept of law is pragmatic, useful as a measure insofar as it serves animal life and
interests but by no means indicative of how nature actually
operates. The validity of a law is functional as "a measure of
events; it is no adequate description of them, much less a
power bringing them about." [43]

The notion of fixed law grows out of animal expectation,
which assumes probability in recurring tropes and then elevates that assumption into a dogmatic law that it foists upon
nature. The law of causality is, he concedes, also "prevalent;"
but neither necessary nor guaranteed as constant. "There is
then no necessity in the relation between cause and effect, and
no assurance that the law is constant. Nevertheless causation
is prevalent; were it not prevalent in fact, the expectation
of it could never have risen." [44] For Santayana, evidence is
no criterion of certainty: "This maxim [of causality] has no
logical cogency, but the presumption it expresses is backed
by a good deal of evidence." [45]

Does nature manifest teleological directions? Not so as to

justify the moral persuasion of final causality, but there is a development of direction out of a "blind disposition, fortified by the fact that circumstances were favorable to that development." [46] It's all a matter of particular forward tensions, determined and modified by the force of lateral tensions which guide the posited dynamic stress of substance. Nature is mechanical, a wonderful machine. [47] Yet existence is irrational, and charges on blindly:

> [It causes] every concretion that can arise to arise, every organism to maintain itself which can maintain itself. Then when any of these concretions collapses, as they must all collapse in turn, it returns to the charge, perhaps in the same direction, like Sisyphus, or, like Proteus, in quite another. In the first case we speak of reproduction, in the second of evolution: but these words do not stand for different forces or principles but only for different results. In reproduction the flux repeats the same trope, in evolution it changes the trope for one more complex or appropriate, imposed by a new balance of forces.[48]

Matter, according to Santayana, is not inert but evidently possesses vital properties capable of spontaneous motion, organization, even life and thought. [49] To protest that matter is incapable of such activity is to argue from some arbitrary notion of matter and "prove dialectically" from this adopted premise that such consequences cannot follow. [50] "What would be thereby proved would not be that matter cannot have the developments which it has, but that that particular idea of matter is wrong or at least inadequate." [51] This is another of Santayana's frequent circles of argumentation. If you do not concede his notion of matter as a first postulate, as a dogmatic premise, then your argumentation will manifest your notion to be wrong since it is not compatible with his notion.

Among the marvelous developments of this dynamic matter is the evolution of a psyche, the biological principle of life in animals.[52] With many metaphorical descriptions and phrases Santayana indicates what he means by psyche.[53] By way of synthesis, we can call it a mode of substance, a trope or habit established in matter which is "inherited or acquired." The consciousness of the psyche is spirit, which consequently "can never be observed as an essence is observed, nor encountered as a thing is encountered. It must be enacted; and the essence of it (for of course it has an essence) can be described only circumstantially and suggested pregnantly. . . ."[54]

The psyche is not identified with spirit; they are definitely distinguished: "By spirit I understand the actual light of consciousness falling upon anything—the ultimate invisible emotional fruition of life in feeling and thought. On the other hand, by the psyche I understand a system of tropes, inherited or acquired, displayed by living bodies in their growth and behavior."[55]

Consciousness, he admits, is a very mysterious manifestation of matter—"the most highly conditioned of existences" and "an overtone of psychic strains, mutations, and harmonies." How does it arise? "At certain junctures animal life, properly a habit in matter, bursts as with a peal of bells into a new realm of being, into the realm of spirit."[56] In other words, minus the flourish of pictorial prose, he says: it just happens. This is as far as a materialistic psychology can go.[57]

Again the great axiom of materialism is adhered to with devout fidelity. All things, even those admittedly immaterial, must be reduced to a material plane: as "habits" or "overtones" of material substance. Santayana has to confess that this "may sound dogmatical."

All origins lie in the realm of matter, even when the being that is so generated is immaterial, because this creation or intrusion of the immaterial follows on material occasions and at the promptings of circumstance. It is safe to say this although it may sound dogmatical, since an immaterial being not grafted in this way upon material events would be undiscoverable; no place, time, or other relations in nature could be assigned to it, and even if by chance it existed it would have to exist only for its own benefit, unreported to anyone else.[58]

And so Santayana completes the circle he has traced as the scope of natural philosophy, which begins with the assumption of material substance only and eventually returns to the rise of intuition of essences in living substances. ". . . if it [natural philosphy] were completed in outline, [it] would come round full circle, and in its account of animals it would report how they came to have intuitions (among them this natural philosophy) and to use them in the description of the world which actually surrounded them." [59] The pivotal point of the cycle is matter, for the "office of matter is precisely to breed mind and to feed it." [60]

Santayana had hinted at this full cycle before he began to explore the realm of matter. In a previous volume he had said:

> The substance of this world is no mere essence . . . it is an existential flux of unknown extent and complexity, which when it falls into certain temporary systems which we call living bodies, kindles intuition there and brings various essences to light, which become terms in belief and knowledge; but substance, although thus posited and symbolized by the animal mind, always remains obscure to it.[61]

Thus, departing from the tight security of intuition of essence and venturing a belief in substance, Santayana identifies this sole substance with matter and attempts to describe the cycle which eventuates in living intuition. Perhaps his report of "how they [animals] came to have this intuition (among them this natural philosophy)" has not been much more than an unexplained statement of fact; but this report has been consistent with his first principle: "the great axiom of materialism." It remains for us to examine his report of the use of these intuitions "in the description of the world which actually surrounds them."

What is the function of essence in the process of knowledge?

Chapter Four

The Role of Essence in Cognition

THE notion of essence was introduced originally as a mediating term in a re-presentative theory of knowledge, the more favored (at least as indicated by the prominence it achieved) of the theories proposed by the school of Critical Neo-Realism.

Yet, as previously noted, Santayana had discussed this notion prior to his contribution to the epistemological studies published by that school in 1920; and afterwards he extensively elaborated this notion by describing its implications and from it developed a whole system of philosophy.

In later years, Santayana discounted the importance of the epistemological aspects of essence, which he described as merely "occasional," and emphasized its ontological aspects. Nevertheless the notion of essence is discovered as the ultimate product of a sceptical and transcendental criticism of knowledge in which it is rooted. The role that essence plays in cognition consequently determines, while more sharply defining, its ontological status. Hence it is important to note the part that essence plays in the process of knowledge, since it is the cognitional key that opens the gates to all of Santayana's realms of being.

ESSENCES ARE NOT KNOWN

If essence alone is evident, as immediately apprehended or intuited, how is anything transitive known? An essence, as we have seen, is not an idea or an image—even though San-tayana often uses these terms indiscriminately in describing the quality of essence. There is no question here of ideal-ism in the sense of ideas being the objects of knowledge. Santayana wishes to avoid the mistake of Berkeley and Hume. Essences are not ideas, nor are they known.[1] The datum of intuition is neither physical nor mental; nor is it an object of knowledge.[2] "The terms of pure thought," he says, "in which observation is couched and in which it rests, I have found to be not thoughts but essences; and the objects of thought, when thought relapses into its animal form of be-lief, are again not thoughts but things." [3]

Intuition of essence, then, is not sensation, either external or internal, nor is it the intellection of an idea. These psychi-cal operations may be the occasion of intuition and the image or idea may manifest an essence. Santayana often mixes his terminology to such an extent that confusion follows and misunderstanding of his drift is an omnipresent danger. But from our analysis of his verbose descriptions of essence we can safely conclude (as we did at the end of Chapter Two) to the concept of essence as a purely logical character, a quidditative quality.

Focusing his attention on this stripped and tenuous quality of things, and presuming it to be the sole datum of conscious-ness, the philosopher then denies any essential difference be-tween sensation and intellection.[4] Yet in practice, in his dis-cussion of the elements of knowledge, Santayana frequently distinguishes these different kinds of perception. His point, however, is that intuition of essence cannot, of itself, make these distinctions and discern the particular mode of stimula-tion that evokes an essence in intuition.

He offers, as an example, the intuition of the essence *yel-low*. If one's eyes are opened and he sees a buttercup, the intuition is called a sensation, but if the subject's eyes are closed the intuition is called an idea (image) or a dream; and if again the subject opens his eyes and sees yellow when there is no buttercup, or any other yellow object, then his intuition is called hallucination. "These various situations," Santayana says, "are curious, and worth distinguishing in optics and in medical psychology, but for the sceptical scrutiny of experience they make no difference." [5] Call the process of intuition what you will, all that is given is an essence—in this instance the essence *yellow.* Intuition is not directly aware of its own form or procedure, nor, for that matter, aware of itself. Intuition is a fact or an event which is posited. [6]

KNOWLEDGE IS FAITH

Essences, then, are not known; nor is intuition itself intuited. [7] Intuition of essence is a simple apprehension of a logical character: of itself non-existent, without assertion or denial which properly pertain to knowledge. What, then, is knowledge? Knowledge, Santayana tells us, is faith. [8] All that is present to intuition, an internal operation of spirit, is some essence. The ambient world is experienced physically by stimulation and shock: in every propulsion or repulsion of the living organism.

The presumption of transitive knowledge is an act of animal faith, the positing of an external object stimulating the animal to instinctive response. Here is the radical dualism, the cognitional dichotomy which Santayana presumes and proposes as the basis of his epistemology. Allowing for, and trying to understand his confusing terminology, we can state that Santayana separates and does not merely distinguish *that which* is known and *that by which* something is known. This division cuts even deeper, as we shall see. The ideal and the real are utterly and irreparably disparate. They represent two separate realms: one of matter contacted, the other of essence intuited. These are expressed by:

(a) "the real contact with things, the cognitive intent, justified by faith, and prompting to inquiry that are proper to *knowledge.*"
(b) "the pictures, emotions, and ideal relations that are proper to imagination." [9]

This marks a fundamental division and total separation between the realm of essence, as the mind internally participates in it, and the realm of matter, which is encountered externally in action. (Here we are speaking of an epistemological separation, not ontological: for material substances also participate in the realm of essence insofar as they assume particular forms.) Knowledge, which is more than pure intuition, since it ascribes external relations and presumes to describe an encountered substance, must be a leap—a leap of faith.

Instinctively, and in a manner natural to spirit, we posit objects encountered by a presumption of animal faith and proceed to describe these objects in terms of essences. This is what Santayana means by knowledge.[10] Any cognitive claim must be an act of faith, for all that is given is an essence, or a pattern of essences: not the constitutive essences of things—somehow seized and apprehended cognitively—but simply logical characters or qualities. The function of essences in cognitive claims is to provide descriptive terms by which we can think and speak about the objects we encounter, and act upon or react to, in the vicissitudes of life.

The Rise of Essence

Before fitting essence into the scheme of knowledge, we should indicate the origin of essences (not that ideal essences are in *some place* before appearing in intuition, since essences do not exist) by determining the causes or occasions of their appearance. This problem might have been posed in Chapter Two to clarify the definition of essence; but because essences pertain to cognition as its expression, we will discuss their origin before assigning their precise function in knowledge.

Since essences are "ideal terms at the command of fancy" they may be invoked in meditation, reverie, or the play of dialectic. They may appear unbidden, spontaneously, to the idle or dreaming mind. Ordinarily, however, they are occasioned by the stimulation exerted by things encountered in action and thereupon serve as signs of those things. The provocation of encountered objects stimulates the evocation of essences by spirit; reverting to these sudden intrusions of essences, spirit may evoke additional essences to describe her delight or wonder or anger. Essences, therefore, elicit types of reaction in spirit, serve to describe these reactions and enable the mind to think and speak about them. Santayana explains:

> What is given becomes in this manner a sign for what is sought and a conventional description of it. . . . If thought arises at all, it must think something after some fashion; and the essences it invokes in intuition enable it to imagine, to assert, and perhaps truly to know something about what is not itself nor its own condition, some existing thing or removed event which would otherwise run on blindly in its own medium, at best overtaking the animal unawares or confronting him to no purpose.[11]

There are two elements present in this contact between spirit and its ambient environment. Something beyond and outside of spirit is encountered by the living organism, which, in turn, responds with the manifestation of an essence to that spirit. This encounter with an object, however, is posited as an occasion rather than a cause of the appearance of the essence.[12]

Santayana vehemently declares that the essences given in intuition are not derived from things external to spirit. Being non-existent, essences cannot cause themselves. Nor are they abstracted from material objects. They are purely internal, he insists, spontaneously invoked:

> The essences given in intuition are fetched from no original. . . . They are dream-lights kindled by my fancy, like all the terms of discourse; they do not need to be previously resident either in the object or in the organ of sense. Not existing at all, they cannot be the causes of their own appearance; nor would introducing an existing triangle under the skin, or making the brain triangular, in the least help to display the triangle to intuition. But if some material thing called a triangle is placed before me at a suitable distance, the essence dear to Euclid will arise in my mind's eye. No essence would ever appear simply because many hypostatic instances of it existed in the world: a living body must create the intuition and blossom into it, evoking some spontaneous image.[13]

The above citation is quoted at length, for it definitely expresses the dichotomy between spirit and the objects of knowledge in Santayana's philosophy. An external object may be simply and solely an occasion for the completely subjective, self-creative intuition of essence. Again he says: "The environment determines the occasions on which intuitions arise, the psyche—the inherited organization of the animal—determines their form. . . ."[14] Why the psyche chooses one essence rather than some other, granting that contact with things is only occasional to essence, is a critical question that is left unanswered.

CORRESPONDENCE OF ESSENCES

How many essences are involved in a cognitional contact? Is there any correspondence between the essence appearing in intuition and that of the object posited in action?

In any instance of spirit there is a given essence, and also the essence of the event of that intuition. "There are accordingly," he says, "two disparate essences exemplified in every instance of spirit; one is the essence of spirit, exemplified *formally* and embodied in the event or fact that at such a moment such an animal has such a feeling; the other is the essence then revealed to that animal, and realized *objectively* (Scholastic sense) or imaginatively in his intuition." [15] But there must be (or ordinarily is) a third essence, also formal: the essence embodied in the material object encountered, which occasions the formal essence of the spiritual event, by which the objective essence is exemplified in intuition.

The event of spirit or consciousness is an essence relative to reflexive knowledge and leads to more intricate complexities. Here we are concerned with direct transitive knowledge. And we should ask if there is any correspondence between the essence given in intuition and the essence embodied in an external object or event, encountered or experienced. This is a crucial question concerning Santayana's theory of knowledge, and the answer to it is an unmistakable *No*. He does say that "in intent, in belief, in emotion, a given essence takes on a value which to pure spirit it could not have." [16] This value, however, is merely symbolic and is not the directly cognitional value of identity between given and intended essences. We do not, he insists, have an intuition of the essences of things. Substances are not revealed by intuition. [17] There is a "diversity of status" between these two instances of essence, which obtains even in the improbable case of accidental identity—a case which, it would seem, could not be recognized even if it happened. But Santayana intends more than a difference of status, as we shall see. He says:

This diversity of status between an essence embodied and the same essence conceived remains complete even when in its two disparate instances the essence is identical; but this is not normally the case. The essences embodied even in the human body and total human career are not such as human imagination can easily conceive; and the essences embodied in the depths and unattainable dimensions of nature escape us altogether.[18]

Does Santayana propose a type of ontologism, a parallelism between embodied and conceived essences? He replies: "If by parallel we understand simply not intermingled I should answer, Yes; but if by parallel we understand running side by side all the way and corresponding throughout, I should say, No." [19] For there is no ideal meeting between mind and matter. The parallelism is irreparably disjunctive, and even a coincidence of an identity of essence, while possible, is highly improbable. There is no apparent way of recognizing this identity even if it should occur. As Santayana says, "Which of the essences conceived by the human mind, if any, may be credited with being the absolute and intrinsic essences of the natural world, is a question to be left to the judgment and modesty of natural philosophers . . . while such coincidence is possible, all essences whatsoever being open to potential intuition, every presumption is against it." [20]

ANTECEDENT SUBJECTIVISM

But Santayana is not concerned with any possible correspondence between intuited and embodied essences. By nature contemplative and by preference solitary, he is content with the internal intuition of essences and tends to scorn their presumed existential counterparts. This attitude is founded upon his subjectivism, radical and complete, which supports his philosophy as an antecedent presumption. Antecedent to all inquiry, he denies veridical value to both sensation and intellection. Desiring to escape the trap of a thorough idealism, he posits a natural world known only by "animal faith." Nature, instinctively posited, gives rise to all things, including psyches which breed spirit. Spirit then falsely presumes subjective experience and claims its verbal description is a carbon copy of the natural world in which these psyches rise. He elaborates this theme:

> Nature, if nature exists at all, is not a hypostasis of essences defined in human discourse; she is the matrix . . . of human nature and human ideas, ideas which by their origin and their function express the sensibility and reactions of the human organism, and nothing else. To suppose that these ideas reproduce and literally define the intrinsic essence of nature is accordingly an illusion: excusable because inevitable in an animal at once active and ignorant. . . .[21]

Santayana's radical subjectivism is expressed by his opinion that ideas (which for him are not essentially different from sensations) "by their origin and function express the sensibility and reactions of the human organism, *and nothing else.*"

Elsewhere he cites an old problem posed by subjectivists: the reverse sensation of a hot hand in cold water and a cold hand in hot water. And he concludes: "Evidences soon accumulate to prove that no quality in the object is like any datum of sense. Nothing given exists. . . . The notion that knowledge is intuition, that it must either penetrate to the inner quality of its object or else have no object but the overt datum, has not been carried out with rigor; if it had it might have been sooner abandoned."[22] Thus Santayana rejects both realism and idealism, while attempting to hold on to both and bridge the trans-subjective gap by an appeal to faith. Nevertheless, subjectivism in his theory of knowledge remains: not as a conclusion but as an antecedent premise presupposed to his radical cognitional dualism.

SOME CONSEQUENCES OF THIS DUALISM

Since immediate apprehension of essence is all that is given, the distinction between sensation and intellection, between the particular and the universal, the abstract and the concrete, are all superfluous distinctions consequently imposed upon things by spirit which actually sees only some essence, itself undistinguished except from every other essence.[23] Actually, in practice, Santayana is forced to make some distinctions among these notions and does so.

The doctrine of essence in his philosophy likewise excuses the philosopher from distinguishing primary from secondary qualities. According to him: "the question of primary and secondary qualities, as mooted in modern philosophy, is a false problem. It rests on the presumption that the data of sense can be and should be constituents of the object in nature, or at least exactly like its constituents." [24]

Symbolic nominalism likewise follows. Essences are signs of things encountered in action. Names may be given either:

(a) *to things:* "like a gesture, designating a natural object without describing it . . . to indicate a thing distinguished by its position relatively to me in the natural world . . . to point to an existence."

(b) *or to essences:* "as for instance, to the triangle or to beauty . . . these names are inaptly called general . . . because they do not designate classes of things, but in designating an essence they leave open the question whether any or many things exist describable by that term. Names then designate not particulars but universals." [25]

"Thus," he continues, "the profit of bestowing names on things and of speaking in prose, like the profit of being sensible at all to external objects, does not lie in revealing the essence of these objects but in expediting action amongst them." [26] Santayana follows up with an example. When the essence of the color of the sky appears to intuition, a different essence immediately follows to describe the original intuition. It may be the word "blue," but it need not be. For, as he says, "the Spanish word *azul* in my case would do just as well; a fact which shows how separate the intuition is in intending from the intuition in seeing, and how disparate." [27]

Things are known only in the sense that they are named, distinguished only roughly and by their occasions. But "they are not known at all in the sense of being disclosed in their inner nature, either totally or partially. The specious essence intuited is *the name* given by the psyche to the material force encountered or exerted; it is a spontaneous symbol, not abstract even its origin. . . ." [28]

Discourse, and dialectic of any kind, consequently lack veridical value in the sense of expressing, relating, or deducing facts. Explanation is simply "the utterance, in further words or images, of relations and terms implied in a given essence: it is the explication of meanings. But facts have no meaning in that sense . . . facts are surds, they exemplify fragments of the realm of essence chosen for no reason." [29]

Dialectic then traces the implication of one essence in another and "can never issue from the eternal world." Things have no dialectical relations, their very existence and fluidity being a defiance to dialectic. Things are always changing and are never the same from one moment to the next. Furthermore, the mind itself so fluctuates that it is doubtful that any term of thought can be repeated exactly as given in its first instance. "Dialectic," he says, "can weave together only eternal essences: and the pattern it thus designs is an eternal essence in its turn. . . . In a mind so volatile as the human, it is not to be expected that the entire complex essence present at one moment should ever be present again. The organ of thought being in flux, the terms of thought can hardly be repeated." [30]

Santayana conceives the psyche as "predetermined at birth to certain generic conceptions and transitions . . . rendered precise and irrevocable by habits formed under the pressure of circumstances." [31] So prejudiced by instinct and habit, spirit makes rash presumptions and becomes embroiled in conflicts of its own making between "reason and fact, desire and event, the ideal and the actual, nature according to philosophers and nature according to nature." [32] No logic can be foisted upon nature. Since essences "have no transitive relations" and all forms of dialectic are subjective patterns of essence, logic merely "expresses the habit and range of the psyche in the thinking animal." [33]

Judgment itself is a bold stroke of animal faith, since it identifies terms in isolation with the same terms in relation. In judgment there is much more than the simple security of intuition, for "there is assumed discourse, involving time, transcendent reference, and various adventitious surveys of identical objects." [34] No demonstration, then, can claim veridical value. Presuming an arbitrary definition of terms agreed upon, a logical demonstration can be made. But the logical relation of the propositions and the proper conclusion from which they are drawn result in logical necessity only. Demonstration, therefore, is only formal and consequently can be correct; but materially it can make no claim to be true. Demonstration of fact, therefore, is a matter of faith:

> The validity of demonstration is accordingly a matter of faith only, depending on the assumption of matters of fact incapable of demonstration. I must believe I noted the terms of the argument separately and successfully if I am to assert anything in identifying them or pronouncing them equivalent,

or if the conclusion in which they appear now is to be relevant in any way to the premises in which they appeared originally.[35]

INTENT IN TRANSITIVE KNOWLEDGE

From the doctrine summarized above, an epistemological dichotomy is evident, a fresh enunciation of Cartesian dualism, only more radical in its thorough consistency. A chasm separates mind and matter, thought and thing—or, in Santayana's terminology, intuited essences and external objects intended in discourse. Essences given in intuition are not identified with extra-mental objects, which are essences embodied in the material world. Again he makes his position clear on this point:

> Essences first and normally manifested in feeling and thought are not the essences that have been embodied multitudinously and successively in things since the beginning of the world, and that now define their dynamic nature . . . ideas are not things but ideas; and ideas, like words, may be excellent signs for events in the field of action, without in the least resembling them . . . the justification required (in asserting true transitive knowledge) is not that the essence given in discourse should repeat the essence embodied in material events—a repetition which is unlikely, superfluous, and incongruous with the summary function of sensation . . . for in naming, reporting, or prefiguring events, discourse will necessarily add an intellective context, a moral perspective, a mocking humor which are not in them.[36]

In true knowledge, therefore, Santayana can (in fact, must) conclude that "the test does not lie in any comparison of the essences invoked by those names and the essences of the existing objects, for since these objects are removed facts their essences cannot be present to intuition." [37] How, then, does he propose to bridge the chasm between the given (essence) and the not-given (existing thing) and measure their relevance in terms of truth?

The leap across the chasm is made by *intent*, by which spirit relates her terms to the object she intends, or means, when attending to or discoursing about that object. The leap is made blindly, for all knowledge of fact is a presumption of animal faith. The object of intent is hidden and merely posited. By uprooting itself from its immediate datum, spirit becomes perception, and perception knowledge. Consciousness, therefore, is "intuition carried by intent" and thereby becoming perception and consequent knowledge.

"And this perception and knowledge are . . . normally and virtually true . . . but true as language may be true, symbolically, pragmatically. . . ." [38] In choosing terms of description "the psyche creates spirit, for they [the terms] are essences given in intuition; and in directing her action or endeavor, backward or forward, upon these remote events, she creates intent in the spirit, so that the given essences become descriptions of the things with which the psyche is then busied." [39]

Now we meet two crucial difficulties. Santayana anticipates them:

(1) But how, I may ask, can intent distinguish its hidden object, so that an image, distorted or faithful, may be truly or falsely projected *there*, or used to describe *it*? How does the spirit divine that there is such an object, or where it lies?

(2) And how can it appeal to a thing which is hidden, the object of mere intent, as to a touchstone or standard for its various descriptions of that object distinguishing degrees of clarity or correctness . . . ? [40]

Santayana immediately continues: "I answer that it does so by animal presumption, positing whatever object instinct is materially disposed to cope with, as in hunger, love, fighting, or the expectation of a future." [41] This reply answers the first inquiry. The object of intent, then, is posited because, as we might put it succinctly, we bump into it; or because we are subjectively disposed to find it there. As we proceed we shall see another element ("bodily attitudes") which posits the object in a particular place, *here* rather than *there*.

There still remains the problem of the criterion of truth. Objects of faith (everything but intuited essences), we are constantly reminded, "can never, even in the most direct perception, come within the circle of intuition." [42] We have no intuition of things, only of non-existent essences; for "even in pure dialectic the comparison is with a datum *believed* to have been given formerly." [43]

What is left? Do we know only ideas? Santayana scorns absolute idealism. Then do we know only essences? No, he insists; we do not *know* essences but apprehend them immediately. Intuition is purely internal, and by knowledge Santayana understands transitive knowledge of external and existent objects and events. [44] How it is possible, then, Santayana very justifiably asks himself, "to posit an object which is not a datum, and how without knowing positively what this object is can I make it the criterion of truth in my ideas?" [45]

This challenge, he admits, is fundamental and easily leads to a dogmatic scepticism which denies the very possibility of knowledge—but only as long as "the assumptions which it makes are not challenged in turn." The principal assumption, under which so many mortals have been laboring and which now poses this problem, is "the assumption that in a true description . . . the terms should be identical with the constituents of the object, so that the idea should *look like* the thing that it knows." [46]

RADICAL DUALISM AND PRAGMATIC TRUTH

Santayana goes on to deny any necessary relation between ideas and things: the chasm is widened rather than bridged. By "bodily attitude" (inclination towards an object sensed) we posit an object in a particular place and fancy finds a name for it.[47] Names may vary: all describe in some convenient and pragmatic way a particular and, as experienced, trans-subjective object; and the chosen name may serve as a suitable symbol for it. The essences which are invoked in intuition on the occasion of contact with things may be named; but these essences cannot be called true except in the sense that it is true that they appear.[48] While truth of judgment is pragmatic, insofar as opinions are suitable to cope with situations, the truth of things is ontological and eternal. The truth, for Santayana, is "the complete ideal description of existence; and any part of this description will be a truth, that is, a part of the truth." [49] That which is true is that which has been, or will be, exemplified existentially, that segment of the realm of essence illustrated in nature. Santayana thereby restricts his notion of truth to an ideal ontological sense, yet unrelated to any intellect measuring or measured by it. He distinguishes between truth and correctness:

(a) the truth properly means the sum of all true propositions, what omniscience would assert, the whole ideal system of qualities and relations which the world has exemplified or will exemplify . . . all things seen under the form of eternity.

(b) the fact is, of course, that an idea can be correct or incorrect only if by the word idea we mean not a datum but an opinion. An opinion is true if what it is talking about is constituted as the opinion asserts it to be constituted.[50]

The problem remains. How, by Santayana's theory of knowledge, can correctness be tested—or, in our own terms, what is the criterion of true judgment or formal certitude? The inevitable conclusion is supplied by Santayana himself: "To test this correctness may be difficult or even impossible in particular cases; in the end we may be reduced to believing on instinct that our fundamental opinions are true. . . ." [51] We not only may but *must*.

We must close our eyes to the chasm that lies between essence and existence and straddle the gap as we work our way through the world blindly—by "animal faith."

Santayana, however, is not concerned with the truth of things—only their ideal essences, which he elevates to an idolatrous primacy.

Chapter Five

The Primacy of Essence

IN LATER years, Santayana complained of the critical emphasis on his doctrine of essence, protesting that "there is now much denunciation of my theory of essence, with some misunderstanding of it, and greater emphasis laid on it than I should lay myself. . . ."[1] The basis of this complaint was that to him essence was obvious and it should be equally obvious to others. If it was not so clear to others it was because the rest of men are so beclouded by conventional opinions they fail to recognize what is closest to them. Santayana considered himself a practical and moral philosopher, seeking only a satisfactory adjustment to those realms of being which he found open to exploration.

This complaint, however, is hardly justified. The notion of essence, defined according to his own epistemological and materialistic prejudices, is the foundation stone of Santayana's whole system of philosophy. And in the last of the realms of being which he treated, that of spirit, he developed a moral and aesthetic way of life that culminates in a naturalistic contemplation of essences for their own sake. The primacy of essence in the construction of his system of philosophy should be evident from our summary exposition of that system. Now we wish to sum up briefly the primacy of essence in its moral aspects, which determines the application of the philosophy of essentialism as a way of life.

The Moral Function of Essence

Matter holds a generative primacy, since it creates spirit; but spirit is the better part of nature to choose. Spirit can look across the chasm to the ambient material world and incline its intentions in that direction as the necessary occasions arise; but spirit is happiest, at least for Santayana, when it closes its eyes and dreams awake. Spirituality may indeed spring from material conditions, but spirit can be self-contemplative and need not become enmeshed in the morass from which she emerged: she can turn to look in another direction—at herself and the essences which come to play in her realm.[2]

Santayana's flight from existence and retreat into solitary contemplation is not without compensation. Essence is better than existence, more secure and in itself undemanding of any pledge of faith in either a natural or supernatural existence. There remains the boundless perspective of a free mind, unfettered by existential claims—and beauty lies beyond, waiting to greet and embrace the pure contemplative.

Materialism does not deny spirituality, but breeds it and feeds it. And essences are not only signals relevant to action. They have a moral function by which they become ends as well as means.[3] Essences are delightful for their own sake. Man can and should rise above the irrational flux of existence and dwell in the realm of spirit, where he can contemplate the infinite variety of essences which appear there. Discourse is poetry, even when it professes to be scientific; and the images aroused by the discursive mind are more valuable than the surds which invoke them.

> Poetry, music and pictures, inspired and shaded by human emotion, are surely better worth having than the inarticulate experience they spring from. Even in our apprehension of the

material world, the best part is the adaptation of it to our position and faculties, since this is what introduces boundaries, perspectives, comparison and beauty.[4]

Spiritualism is not alien to a frank and disinfected naturalism. In his youth, Santayana had bewailed poetically the loss of the glorious ideals of supernatural faith. Later on, however, he developed a compromise by which these ideals might be retained while thoroughly naturalized. But they had to be uprooted from the existential order and transformed into pure ideals, logical forms unrealizable except as purely mental goals. Thus he sought the fruits of religious experience without the dogmas of a supernatural faith.[5] His morality, then, would be purely natural, proper to man as he conceives him: an organism with evolved spiritual perspectives, generated by the mysterious but assuredly materialistic forces of nature. For "only a morality frankly relative to man's nature is worthy of man, being at once vital and rational, martial and generous; whereas absolutism smells of fustiness as well as of faggots." [6]

THE PROCESS OF SPIRITUAL PERFECTION

How is this ideal natural moral life achieved? By the perfection of spirit through its proper and perfect function; and "the perfect function of spirit is pure intuition." [7] Santayana's kingdom is not of this world: it lies in the realms of essence and spirit.

Matter provokes forms, and the waiting and watchful spirit can seize them in an intuition of their essences and contemplate their inert, unassertive beauty and truth. For, like the soul in Aristotle's doctrine, spirit is potentially all things; and therein lies its freedom and glory.

The freedom and glory of spirit come from its impotence; by its impotence it is guiltless, by its impotence it is universal, by its impotence it is invulnerably supreme. Its essence is to be light, not to be power; and it can never be pure light until it is satisfied with an ideal dominion, not striving to possess or to change the world, but identifying itself only with the truth and beauty that rise unbidden from the world into the realm of spirit.[8]

This passive contemplation of essence ignores rather than denies existence. Santayana's partiality towards Indian philosophy is apparent, even without his many assertions of it. But he will not deny the rampaging flux; rather, he wills to rise above it. Existence is "terrible" and the spiritual man must climb above and beyond it and survey it from afar, freed from its claims in the unassertive security of intuition, where it partakes of the eternity of pure essence.[9]

There is a spiritual struggle to be achieved by the novice who would renounce the dictatorial demands of existence and follow the flight of free spirit. The religious motif becomes apparent, and Santayana proceeds to appropriate the terms of Christian dogma and morality and apply them to his own naturalistic doctrine.

Spirit must free itself from the snares of the three-fold enemy: the flesh, the world, and the devil. Enslavement to carnal desires distracts spirit from her vocation; so also does worldliness, with its absorbing possessiveness. The devil, according to Santayana, is a symbolic figure for pride of power and knowledge. All such distractions of spirit must be overcome in order to obtain the freedom which is conducive to aesthetic contemplation.[10] Spirit in its fight for freedom must suffer, albeit innocently, and that is the true significance of the Cross. Salvation is possible only through suffering, but the goal that beckons is a fresh rising of spirit above all conflicting and divided interests—the Resurrection.

There are three stages in Santayana's naturalistic version of the perfection of spiritual life: Distraction, Liberation,

Union. In the dark night of the soul, as described by St. John of the Cross, the appropriating philosopher recognizes the self-surrender necessary to attain a purified and liberated natural spirit. The faith required during this dark night is not a supernatural faith in any revealed dogma.[11] It is *"fides caritate formata,"* which means "trust that beyond that blank negation and inner death which utter self-surrender involved there would come in the end a positive liberty, a clear vision, a living flame of love." [12] The love achieved, true charity, is a benevolent and tolerant complacency that recognizes the relative perfection of all things, even in their grossest imperfections, and an ideal union with them.

The Nature of Spiritual Union

What is the union which culminates this spiritual life, as its fruit and flower and ultimate perfection? It is not a union with a divine Person, nor, for that matter, with any other substance. "The union sought by a liberated spirit is no fusion of its substance with any other substance, but a moral unanimity of fellowship with the life of all substances in so far as they support or enlarge its own life." [13]

The expected conclusion is that "mystic union resides in intuition; it is not a union of objects or with objects, but a synthesis reached in life and expressed in a given quality of feeling. This is a feeling of union and bliss. . . ." [14] Essence approaches the peak of its primacy. Pure intuition of essence (admittedly difficult to sustain, yet affording some moments of bliss) is raised to the level of the only and the ultimate human beatitude. Hence, "life triumphant is life transmuted into something which is not life—into union with essence, with so much of the eternal as is then manifested in the transitory." [15]

This union, which "is achieved . . . by intellectual worship," promotes the only peace possible to mankind. Spirit, in the repose of its blissful union with essence, can forget itself in the joy of its pure ecstatic vision. A naturalistic version of sanctity is possible:

> Then to the spirit that has renounced all things, all things are restored: and having renounced itself also, it cannot resist any inspiration or think evil of any good, but embraces them all in the eternal object of its worship, not as they may have existed in the world in passing and in conflict, but as they lie ideally reconciled in the bosom of the Good, at peace at last with themselves and with one another.[16]

Essence ascends. For now essences are "objects of worship."

THE TRINITY OF NATURE

All things, including Christian revelation, are reducible to the doctrines of Santayana's philosophy. "My treatment of these four realms of being may be regarded as a reduction of Christian theology and spiritual discipline to their secret interior source. In particular my analysis transposes the doctrine of the Trinity into terms of pure ontology and moral dialectic." [17] By this ill-chosen extension of his appropriation of Christian terminology, Santayana dissolves the Trinity into his own naturalistic philosophy. Father, Son and Holy Ghost are transposed into Matter, Essence and Spirit. He explains in detail:

> This assault of reality, in the force of whatsoever exists or happens, I call matter or the realm of matter; but evidently this very power is signified by the First Person of the Trinity, the Father, almighty creator of heaven and earth and of all things visible and invisible.
>
> Yet all things, according to the Nicene creed, were perforce created through the Son; and this dogma which might seem unintelligible, becomes clear if we consider that power could not possibly produce anything unless it borrowed some form

from the realm of essence and imposed that form on itself and on its works. Power would be annulled before it began to exert itself unless it did or produced something specific, something eternally distinct and recognizable in its character. The Son is thus an indispensable partner and vehicle for the life of the Father.[18]

Following the Nicene creed, he notes that "the Son was *begotten not made*, that is to say, came through an inner impulse, without plan or foresight, from the substance of the Father; as in nature it is absurd to imagine that the shape taken by things was an aim pursued in their taking it." [19] He continues:

> If we interpret in this way the Father to be power and the Son to be form, we see at once how the essence or quality of each is independent and incomparable, while their existence is one and inseparable. To exercise power is to select and adopt form: by which selection or adoption power ceases to be a merely explosive and empty strain, and form ceases to be an infinite undiscriminated field of possibilities.
>
> In its own direction essence is entirely irrelevant to existence, equally necessary in every part, yet only logically necessary. But by the intervention of irrational power (as for instance in the propensity or compulsion to think) the infinity of essence is determined to a particular complex or series of forms of existence at large. This complex or series of forms exemplified in the universe composes the truth about it; and this is the side of reality approachable by the intellect. It is the Logos, comparable with the heaven of Platonic Ideas, with the God of Aristotle, and with *nous*, the second hypostasis in the trinity of Plotinus.[20]

The peak of the primacy is reached. Essence, as it is irrationally determined by exemplification, is God.

THE RELIGIOUS SIGNIFICANCE OF ESSENCE

The notion of essence is thus developed to the point of divinization, and Santayana admits that his philosophy is "a discipline of the mind and heart, a lay religion." [21] In a paper entitled "Ultimate Religion," [22] which he read in the *Domus Spinozana* at the Hague, on the occasion of the tercentenary commemoration of the birth of his fellow philosopher and kindred soul, Benedict de Spinoza, Santayana proposed an ultimate religion "proper to a wholly free and disillusioned spirit"—a recognition and respect for universal power, the love of universal good, allegiance towards universal truth, worship of perfection and beauty.

During the closing years of his life he retained his attachment for the essence of revealed religion, without acknowledging its existential reality. The dichotomy between essence and existence was so thorough that he published a study on *The Idea of Christ in the Gospels*,[23] dwelling only on the idea of the divine in man, as exemplified in the Person of Jesus Christ,—a Person, however, poetically inspired and expressing in myth the naturalism that Santayana himself proposes.

In the last book that he wrote, he defined religion as "the recognition of the Powers on which our destiny truly depends, and the art of propitiating those Powers and of living, as far as the power in us avails, in devout harmony with them." [24] This definition, he believed, covered all forms of religion, including his own, and thus vindicated his proposition that naturalism is not necessarily irreligious.

The circle, and the system, is completed. In the beginning of this exposition, as a principal part of its background, we called attention to the undeniably strong influence of religion and solitude in the development of Santayana's philosophy of essence. This thesis is justified, even without critically pointing it out at length. It is eloquently expressed throughout Santayana's writings.

His earliest writings were poems expressing his disillusionment with revealed religion and the hope of finding solace and solution in nature. His third published book [25] set a theme that he tenaciously clung to through every other work: religion, presumed to have its source in divine revelation, is merely a symbolic expression of naturalistic ideals. He proceeded to develop this thesis into a supporting system of philosophy, which rested on a foundation of materialism and radical epistemological dualism. *Scepticism and Animal Faith* proposed a sceptical method and the discovery of essence. The subsequent *Realms of Being* enlarged that concept through its implications and made it the focal point of a naturalistic interpretation of religion.

The drift was obvious in the first volume, the *Realm of Essence*. For although he had disclaimed all systems of philosophy as "taught only . . . by individuals setting out to be prophets" he proceeded to develop his own system of philosophy into a "lay religion"—and in the early fervor of the volume on essence he declared enthusiastically: "I think that a religion is possible which should have pure Being for its object, and that it might even become a popular cult." [26]

And who is its prophet?

Part III—Criticism

It is honor enough to be read and studied, even if only to
be combated; and I send my critics back to their respective
camps with my blessing, hoping that the world may prove
staunch and beautiful to them, pictured in their own terms.

GEORGE SANTAYANA
Apologia Pro Mente Sua

Introductory Note

On Critical Procedure

A SERIOUS difficulty arises in any attempt to subject Santayana's notion of essence to a thorough examination. Since essence is the foundation of his system of philosophy, it follows, granting some consistency in his elaboration of this notion, that essence is immediately related to every part of that system. Consequently a thorough analysis of essence in Santayana's philosophy requires a complete criticism of the whole of his philosophy. Obviously this would be too ambitious a project, at least within the limits of a single volume. A more confined and restricted approach, therefore, is necessary.

This brings us immediately to a choice of critical procedure, before discussing certain intrinsic difficulties.

An external, comparative criticism is possible in which the notion of essence and other fundamental notions in Santayana's system of philosophy can be compared to the same or similar notions in another philosophical synthesis. This has been done already, and creditably, in an examination of Santayana's philosophy relative to the principles of Thomistic philosophy.[1]

An alternative procedure is to concentrate on a critique of Santayana's epistemological principles. He is a principal representative of a school of epistemological thought, the school of Critical Neo-Realism; furthermore, the notion of essence played a prominent role in the solution to the critical problem that was proposed by that school. Moreover, whatever solution is given to this problem, as the problem is raised in modern philosophy, determines the whole content of a philosophy based on that solution. The epistemological basis of Santayana's philosophy is, accordingly, fundamental; it has not been overlooked either, for a study of this basis has been undertaken.[2]

For my own part, I wish to attempt an intrinsic criticism and concentrate on the notion of essence: touching upon, without exploring extensively, its most pertinent implications. Proceeding intrinsically, I intend to follow Santayana's own procedure by examining as briefly as possible: (a) the method by which he discovers essence; (b) the term of that method, essence itself; and (c) the function of essence, particularly in cognition.

In attempting this intrinsic criticism I shall appeal, as Santayana did, to the sound orthodoxy of common sense. Frequently he insisted that he founded his doctrine on common sense experience;[3] and so on that basis he invites criticism and an evaluation of his opinions.

No critic can exercise judgment without employing definite principles which enlighten his vision. Common sense, as merely popular and unscientific opinion, is not enough. Santayana, however, sometimes professed himself to be a Scholastic "at heart" and "in principles," and to William James he attributed the remark: "Scholasticism was nothing but common sense carried out consistently."[4] That Scholastic philosophy is a consistent and scientific elaboration of common sense principles is true. To that philosophy I am committed, not as to a closed system but to its sound development of reasonable conclusions deduced from the very first principles of thought and being, always capable of further explication and application. Santayana may count himself among us "at heart," not, however, "in principles."

While holding to the Thomistic development of Aristotelian philosophy, recognizing it as a scientific synthesis founded on common sense principles, I do not intend to invoke the authority of its proponents, founders or followers, other than: (a) to clarify occasionally the sources from which Santayana borrows many of his terms without their original signification, (b) to point out that many of his "discoveries" are not original, and (c) to provide a clearer expression of a point than I am able to make myself.

The primary intrinsic difficulty in criticizing Santayana's doctrine is his ornamented literary form, a source of artistic charm and scientific confusion. A scientific thinker cannot afford the luxury of lush, florid prose and hope to express his thought with precision. But Santayana says: "My philosophy neither is nor wishes to be scientific; not even in the sense in which, in temper and method, the *Summa* of St. Thomas might be called scientific." [5]

Santayana was a poet before he was a philosopher, and brought to his formal philosophy poetical expression. He may deny that these are conflicting offices in the interpretation of nature; but the philosopher's vision is intellectual and his expression of it rational and literal; while the poet sees things imaginatively and speaks fancifully and in metaphors. Unfortunately Santayana preferred fancy to reason and the impulsive flight of imagination to the planned plodding of demonstration. He achieves, as his critics are fond of pointing out, "flashes of insight" in particular instances; but he is, by his own admission, too impatient to develop these insights from the principles from which they spring through their implications to logical conclusions. He confesses that this obstacle has often hindered a proper understanding of his views:

> That they should often be misunderstood is rather my fault,
> because I have clothed them in a rhetoric that, though per-

fectly spontaneous and inevitable in my own thoughts, misleads at first as to their character. . . . I detest disputation and distrust disproofs. Nor do I expect or desire that everybody should think as I do.[6]

This final protest of indifference to criticism he frequently expressed.[7] But as a difficulty facing a critic it is superficial. The reader often gets the impression that Santayana protests too much. No matter what his terms, clothed in colorful rhetoric or not, these terms do signify philosophical interpretation and are subject to critical analysis.

Santayana himself hopes to dodge behind his own sceptical method and his transcendentalism. He says: "The sceptic is not committed to other men's language; nor can he be convicted out of his own mouth by the names he is obliged to bestow on the details of his momentary vision." [8] This attempt to escape, however, is futile. Santayana speaks intelligibly, albeit rhetorically, and the opinions he proposes to base upon common sense can be challenged on the very same basis. No sceptic, as Santayana himself discovered, can linger long in a false "solipsism of the living moment" and refrain from positive assertions, including, at least implicitly, an approval of the transcendentalism which achieves that solipsism. Santayana's positive assertions can, if need be, be challenged positively.

Nor is it sufficient to appeal to logical consistency without any claim to truth. He asks himself:

"All that you yourself have written, here and elsewhere, about essence, is it not true?" "No, I reply, it is not true, nor meant to be true. It is a grammatical or possibly a poetical construction having, like mathematics or theology, a certain internal vitality and interest; but in the direction of truth-finding, such constructions are merely instrumental like any language or any telescope." [9]

While disclaiming truth in his philosophy and professing a free and unfettered mind, Santayana here speaks about essence, a logical character, and makes no mention of matter—whether or not the great axiom of materialism is true—and yet he manages to deny existential truth to the foundations of theology, equating its terms with mathematical possibilities. Furthermore this demure pretense to deny a claim to truth is not always so manifest in his writings. Elsewhere he speaks more boldly: "My philosophy is justified, and has been justified in all ages and countries, by the facts before every man's eyes; and no great wit is requisite to discover it, only . . . candour and courage."[10] Whether his philosophy fits the facts or not remains to be seen—and, incidentally, this is a curious boast from one who can claim no knowledge of fact at all, only uncertain faith.

He admits to have "often clouded my . . . terms with useless or disturbing allusions" yet insists that "my propositions will be logically necessary, being deducible from the definitions or intuitions of the chosen terms, and especially of this chosen term 'essence' itself."[11] And upon the completion of his construction of a system of philosophy, he was forced to admit that it did not "escape being, in effect, a system of the universe."[12] Thus Santayana ended up by contradicting the emphatic proposition contained in the introductory volume to his system of philosophy: "My system, accordingly, is *no system of the universe*."[13]

If Santayana did, as he finally admitted, articulate a system of philosophy about the universe; and proceeded from common sense principles and experience, as he claims, then his system of philosophy is subject to the criticism of any other philosopher, who thereupon may agree, with commendation, or disagree, proposing reasonable objections.

Our specific task is to work from the "chosen term," from which, Santayana says, all his other propositions are deducible. Proceeding logically, a chapter will be devoted to method, Santayana's approach to and discovery of essence; then the term essence, itself, will be examined. Finally, the function of essence, in nature, cognition, and the spiritual life, will be subjected to criticism. It will be tempting, though impossible, to explore the many avenues opening up along the way, inviting critical exploration; but at least general directions and consequences can be indicated.

Santayana reduced all knowledge to belief. He said: "I think it reasonable to suppose that the beliefs that prove inevitable for me, after absolutely disinterested criticism, would prove inevitable also to most human beings." [14] Perhaps he would not consider this criticism disinterested, accusing me of "private interests," counting me among those weighted down by "superstition" and caught in an adamant loyalty to a "system" (other than his). I intend, however, a criticism, that is sincere (if not possibly disinterested) and based upon common sense (his own basis).

We shall see if these beliefs "prove inevitable also to most human beings"—a category in which, I trust, I can be included without prejudicial labels.

Chapter One

Method

THE first step in a critical analysis of Santayana's notion of essence is to examine the method which terminates in its discovery.

Having considered the conflicts encountered by Santayana in his personal and philosophical background, we are not surprised to find him in the middle span of his life setting out to construct a system of philosophy which would serve as a "discipline of mind and heart" and founding that system upon scepticism. One of Santayana's teachers once told him that he had "Hume in his bones." [1] Like Hume, he plunged into philosophy at the turn of another revolution in its hectic career.

The revolt against idealism was stirring at the turn of the century, although realism's rebellion in England and America did not advance to a critical refutation until Santayana had nearly completed his teaching tenure at Harvard. In his student days, however, he came under the influence of James and Royce, early antagonists in the growing conflict.

The romantic rationalism of the 19th century, paralleling the rise of empiricism which accompanied the advances made in the physical sciences, fostered a distrust of speculative knowledge and a despair of certitude. With the rejection of metaphysics and the successive re-examination of physical hypotheses in the experimental sciences, it is no wonder that Santayana, caught up in this vortex, should decide to step aside, view the possibilities, and make a fresh start.[2]

His mind, however, was by that time too settled in definite opinions and fixed habits of thought to be subjected to a thorough housecleaning. Some of the clutter was sure to be overlooked or considered too precious to be thrown away. He chose scepticism in its extreme form, though not without precious reservations, and threw in his lot with Kant's transcendental criticism. Introspection would be his retreat and the vantage point from which he would survey the field open to philosophy: an understandable choice, considering his background and temperament; an unfortunate one, considering the inevitable consequences.

Curiously, however, we find this introspective philosopher *par excellence*, frequently professing his preference for allegiance to the early Greek philosophers. "I should like to turn to the ancients," he says, "and breathe again a clean atmosphere of frankness and honor." [3] He calls them "original observers of life and nature" and the "best" of all philosophers. Yet he himself chose the musty atmosphere and distorted vision of introspection, observing not nature but himself, and he manifests much more the spirit of the moderns, particularly Descartes, Hume, Kant and Hegel, than he does that of the ancients.

Santayana's preference for the Greeks, therefore, is partial, restricted almost exclusively to Democritus, the venerable father of materialism and sceptical predecessor of the Sophists. It is to the primitive period in Greek philosophy that Santayana turns, not to its golden age of reason's profound conquest of reality. In this latter period, reflecting his own impatience with metaphysics, he finds the Greek thinkers, beginning with Socrates, "rhetoricians." [4] Materialism, scepticism, naturalistic morality: these, Santayana's own tenets, he finds acceptable wherever he discovers them. But metaphysics, according to his own doctrine, is an "hypostasizing" of essences and therefore unwelcome, especially when it presumes to conclude to unmoved movers and reasons to the soul coming "from without the gates."

REJECTION OF FIRST PRINCIPLES

Santayana begins to philosophize (in the later development of his system) by deciding that "a philosopher is compelled . . . to plunge in *medias res*." [5] There are no first principles, he declares, from which any discourse can proceed. Why? Because:

> They can never be discovered, if discovered at all, until they have been long taken for granted, and employed in the very investigation which reveals them . . . in discovering them, and deducing the rest from them, they must first be employed unawares, if they are principles lending cogency to actual discourse . . . they are arbitrary and merely instinctive.[6]

That the first principles of reasoning are employed in every intellectual inquiry, involving any judgment whatsoever, even regarding these principles themselves, is perfectly true—precisely because these principles are first, or ultimate, in the logical order by which the intellect naturally proceeds. This logical order pertains to reasoning from premises to conclusions. Unless there was an absolutely first judgment in this direct order, an ultimate judgment itself undemonstrable because it is self-evident, there could be no judgments at all, an argumentative regress into infinity not only being impossible but incapable of providing any foothold for any demonstration. In the psychological order of knowledge, by which sensation precedes intellection and simple apprehension precedes judgment, there is no question of a first principle except in an originative sense.

First principles are "taken for granted" in the sense that they are always *implicit*, even in simple experiential judgments which psychologically precede intellectual judgment. They are not "arbitrary," because they are founded ontologically in being itself. They are "instinctive" in every human being insofar as the mind possesses them virtually or habitually from the beginning of one's cognitive life. This does not mean that they are innate, for their self-evidence is immediately seized by the intellect from the experience of being. Only in this sense they are said to "come to nature, and are known naturally."

Now a denial of first principles, most obviously the principle of contradiction (which is strictly first and from which the others are immediately inferred [7]), is impossible in practice and irrational as a theory. Even those who presume to philosophize otherwise, cannot fail to exercise these principles, recognized in common sense experience, when they cease to talk folly. Certitude rests upon these principles and a denial of them in no way affects their necessary use for precisely that purpose, for, as a scholar in the field recently stated:

> Even the workings of science presuppose at least the existence of certitude. In every investigation it is taken for granted, for example, not only that contradictories cannot both be true, but that every phenomenon must have a cause, that nature operates in a uniform manner, etc. Without such assumptions (and they are by no means groundless), all experimentation becomes blind groping in the dark with instruments whose accuracy and even existence is always open to doubt. If we cannot be sure that a microscope is not the same as a telescope, we might as well toss a coin to determine which we shall use for the investigation of bacteria. Nor can it be main-

tained that we can *act* on probability as if it were certitude. Such an attitude is a psychological fiction which is impossible to maintain in practice, as even Hume found.[8]

Santayana, as we shall see, also finds this fiction impossible to maintain in practice, and even the "speculative security" which he professes it affords is based upon an unsceptical presumption of transcendental intuition.

Hence in the epistemological order, which is more pertinent to the present discussion, the necessity of first principles imposes itself by self-evidence and is manifested by a reduction to absurdity of any refusal to accept them. Aristotle provides illustrations, using this line of indirect proof to establish first principles of thought and being.[9] Santayana himself, since he chooses to deny the validity of first principles, subjects himself to the absurd irrationalism that such a position entails. The impossibility of proposing or practicing universal scepticism rests upon the infallible truth of the principle of contradiction. Santayana must contradict himself or remain mute altogether. He has written more than thirty volumes.

SCEPTICISM, IMPURE AND SHORT-LIVED

Santayana claims to use a method of ultimate scepticism, doubting all things that are possible to doubt. He recognized the weakness of Descartes, whose doubt was not at all universal or extended. And so he proposes to "push scepticism as far as I logically can, and endeavor to clean my mind of illusion, even at the price of intellectual suicide." [10] But how logical is this endeavor, honestly, and what does he decide are illusions and what are not? Does he, in the end, pay the price of intellectual suicide?

We can follow this endeavor briefly, for we have only a few steps to go.

He pledged himself to common sense and a respect for the "shrewd orthodoxy that the sentiment and practice of laymen maintain everywhere." Yet he immediately disparages the philosophy of the common man, and his first attack is upon religion, deciding against, and not merely doubting, its foundation in truth.[11] The claims of religious faith are not held in abeyance by doubt; they are definitely rejected by an appeal to "mere experience" and "good sense." But the experience and good sense of others, historically the vast majority of men, manifest a contrary judgment. An honest sceptic doubts and suspends judgment until he discovers a basis for certitude. Santayana is a bit precipitous, to say the least.

Two pages later we have suddenly and inexplicably come to a "solipsism of the present moment"; and after another two pages we have arrived at a subjective phenomenalism that regards ideas as arbitrary signs, become "beliefs" in action. Santayana is a very impulsive sceptic and cannot hold his breath as long as Descartes, whose "mind," he declared, "was not plastic nor mystic enough to be profoundly sceptical." [12] Santayana condemns Descartes for holding on to the principle of sufficient reason, as well as eliminating faith and morals from subjection to doubt, yet he himself enters into scepticism weighted down with radical presuppositions which determine the whole course of his subsequent philosophy. Scepticism, if anything, is a game; and Santayana does not play fairly.

I will return to Santayana's own first principles, his dogmatic presuppositions. As for his scepticism, it is sham and folly, a "violent pose" as he admits it to be. Nor is it "invincible" speculatively, for it is based upon false transcendentalism: an unnatural, and really impossible, detachment of existence from the immediate datum of consciousness, a mental trick possible only by abstraction and reflection upon logical entities. He falls into the same trap which ensnared Kant whom he verbally flails.[13] Paul Valery's penetrating analysis of Descartes is applicable, at least in part, to Santayana:

> The question of certitude, or negatively scepticism is . . . a question so positively theoretical that one wonders inwardly whether it is not purely verbal. We all give ourselves a great deal of trouble to convince ourselves that we are dreaming when we are not. But in this case the effort is to extend to everything of which we are aware the suspicion that it is all fully as vain and deceitful as the fantasies of sleep or other wanderings of the mind. Thus the thinker does not hesitate to conclude that we dwell in a world of appearances, and from this follow many deductions of no positive effect in our daily lives. Whether or not we are deluded, whether or not we dream, in no way changes our feelings or our actions. Yet it would seem that taking this position is essential to philosophy; it allows the philosopher to decree *reality* for whatever he chooses, for whatever the fantasies of his thinking suggest to him.
>
> And yet we must worst his artificial doubt, this residue of tradition, which I call artificial because it requires an act of the will, just as it requires language even to make an appearance. In the last analysis it assumes that we have the notion of an operation or transformation which, when applied to pure knowledge of things, will substitute therefor a reality of a second order and will change into the memory of a dream everything we have practically, naturally, and ordinarily held to be real. The statistical weight in favour of reality in its ordinary meaning is crushing.[14]

Reality, in its primary meaning, refers to that which actually exists. Indeed the weight in its favor is crushing, precisely because the existent, and not a mere "logical character," is self-evident. Santayana will tell us that "every assertion about existence is hazarded" and that it rests "on animal faith, not on logical proof." This is a gratuitous assertion, to which we reply that it rests upon common sense experience and obviously cannot be *proven* logically since it is self-evident.

The Futility of Scepticism

Scepticism, in the sense of a recognition of difficulties to be solved and a resolution of false arguments to their implicit contradictions, serves a purpose, indeed a necessary one. St. Thomas points out that those who seek truth without first considering doubt are like people who don't know where they are going; because the exclusion of doubt is the very purpose of a seeker of truth, just as a particular destination is ordinarily intended by a person setting out on a walk. Obviously the stroller who does not know where he is going will never get to any particular place directly. So, too, no one can proceed directly to truth unless he first sees the doubt to be dissolved.[15] Aquinas, therefore, begins all his inquiries into the truth of a proposition by first considering the difficulties or opinions proposed pro and con.

But absolute scepticism, as proposed by Santayana, including a denial of first principles, is an absurd and untenable position, a method altogether futile because of its impossibility. In any judgment whatsoever, something is asserted, thus distinguishing assertion from denial and that which is asserted from its contradictory. The certainty of the principle of contradiction is proclaimed in the very denial of it. Furthermore, in positing doubt, any doubt at all, the ability of the mind to know something is both recognized and exercised; for at least the doubt and its motive, implying also a criterion of truth, are known.

Whether what is known is extra-mental or merely internal phenomena is another question, reserved to critical reflection though implicitly answered in the primary proposition. But the essential ordination of knowledge to an object known is obvious enough to border on the tautological; and here again the questioning of the certainty of this fact proclaims it.

Likewise, in the very exercise of doubt there is implicit certitude of the existence of the subject doubting.

Self-existence, however, is not the first or primitive certitude, as Descartes proposed. The mind is *implicitly* aware of itself thinking, but *explicitly* of thinking *something;* hence, as St. Thomas points out [16] the intellect is conscious of itself through its operation, or exercise; and these operations necessarily are specified by, or terminated in, the objects of its operations. Direct knowledge precedes indirect or reflexive knowledge. We know that we know precisely in our act of knowing something not ourselves.

It is an idle and useless task to chase through the text of Santayana's scepticism, indicating the necessary presence of these inevitable certitudes (the principle of contradiction, the essential function of the mind to know, and self-existence) even in his denials of them. He admits himself that scepticism is only an exercise, and indeed it is: an exercise in mental gymnastics. His fictitious denial of change, memory, and existing facts is possible only by a false transcendentalism or deliberate abstraction. At least Santayana recognizes the futility of proposing scepticism as a dogma:

> Scepticism may thus be carried to the point of denying change and memory, and the reality of all facts. Such a sceptical dogma itself would have to be entertained, and that event would be a fact: and the sceptic in framing that dogma discourses, vacillates, and lives in the act of contrasting one assertion with another—all of which is to exist with a vengeance. Yet this false dogma that nothing exists is tenable intuitively and, while it prevails, is irrefutable.[17]

The last remark that "nothing exists . . . is irrefutable" is based upon a reflexive and abstract consideration, as we shall see. Santayana involves himself in an altogether artificial position, the true character of which he does not seem to grasp. By merely abstracting essence from existence he presumes that he has achieved an actual separation, so that he looks upon an utterly specious essence that has no intrinsic relationship to the existence from which it is abstracted. He thereupon imagines himself free to form beliefs about existence to accommodate his experience with the "shock" of it. He must admit that "a theoretical refusal to trust natural philosophy cannot absolve the most sceptical of us from framing one, and from living by it. I *must* conceive a surrounding world, even if in reflection I say to myself at every step: Illusion, Illusion." [18] His idealistic fate is indicated by his talking about "conceiving" a world; and idealism, which he thought he was avoiding, is precisely where he ends, engulfed in the torrent of his own introspection and struggling to find a lifeline to reality through "animal faith."

Santayana's Dogmatism

Santayana thought there was a choice between dogmatism and scepticism. There is not, however, as he soon discovered and had to admit. To pretend universal scepticism is a fictitious pose, contradictory as a doctrine and practically impossible. Any doctrine implies dogma in so far as it proclaims positive judgments; and even a nugatory nihilism is reducible, or convertible, to positive dogmatism. There can be no question of denying dogma, only the assertion of another one. Santayana recognized this fact himself:

> Dogma cannot be abandoned; it can only be revised in view of some more elementary dogma which has not yet occurred to the sceptic to doubt; and he may be right in every point of his criticism, except in fancying that his scepticism is radical and that he is altogether a sceptic.[19]

Santayana had his own dogmas, and in practice he employs the first principles of thought which he rejected. He even uses them intentionally, speaking of "self-contradiction" [20] and telling us "the soul *causes* the body to grow. . . ." [21] (italics mine.) In applying a notion of identity to his essences [22] he is using the principle of contradiction and the principle of identity, distinguishing essences from nothing and from each other. By his transcendental criticism he can deny existence to the datum of consciousness only by previously knowing it, abstracting from a consideration of it, and then deciding that this abstracted essence, or at least a distinguished essence, is the primitive datum.

Scepticism must eventually halt and give way to the positive assertion that something is self-evident. For Santayana, this sole self-evident object of intuition is an essence, in origin as well as status altogether subjective and intramental—a monstrously gratuitous assertion, contrary to common sense experience to which the philosopher pretended to adhere. The datum, Santayana repeatedly tells us, is "by definition the whole of what is found" [23] in immediate intuition; "by hypothesis, [it] is the whole of what solicits my attention." [24] But whose definition, whose hypothesis is he referring to? His own, according to which existence is not "included in any immediate datum," [25] since existence implies external or "adventitious relations." [26] How is he able to judge between external and internal relations, and how can he deny external relations unless he first abstracts from them? This cardinal presumption is dogmatism in gigantic proportions.

The primary principles and gratuitous dogmas of Santayana's whole philosophy may be reduced to two *a priori* postulates: materialism as to the origin of all things, and a radical transcendentalism as an epistemological method. [27] Santayana, who claimed to be "the only sceptic living" was not a sceptic at all. From his own two primary principles flow inevitably his naturalism and "essentialism"—the latter a vain attempt to avoid outright idealism by making his essences symbols rather than objects of knowledge and positing the external world as a presumption of "animal faith." Naturalism must be true *a priori*,[28] as well as the irrationality of existence; hence fancy is preferable to fact, and pragmatism and personal interests become the criteria of what is founded in existence and what is not.

That the real was rotten and only the imaginary at all interesting seemed to me axiomatic . . . it is still what I think. It is by no means an artificial academic hypothesis; it doesn't appeal at all to the professors; it is a system of presuppositions and categories discovered already alive and at work within me willy-nilly, like existence itself, and virtually present not only in the boy but in the embryo.[29]

Materialism cannot be both an arbitrary belief—which it certainly is, and by Santayana's own philosophical principles —and a valid, minimum, and *a priori* presupposition with which we must all start.

Santayana straddles antinomies in a most embarrassingly unsceptical manner. His materialism, which he has no right, or even possibility, to propose in the light of his own principles, somehow produces an utter immaterialism. He must "register the emergence of consciousness in animal bodies," he says, "as a brute fact." [30] No evidence is offered, only lush metaphorical descriptions of a psyche conceiving intuition (aptly described as "a miracle child") by a "warm ray from the sun or from some other celestial source." [31]

If materialism is evident enough to become a presupposition, then nothing immaterial is evident or, for that matter, even possible. Conversely, if an immaterial essence is all that is certain, then a postulate of materialism is the rashest presumption possible—at the very opposite pole of credibility.

If Santayana were consistent in his transcendentalism he would remain there and follow his predecessors with more logic to absolute idealism. Yet by a blind, groping instinct of animal faith, he leaps to the antipodes and pledges himself to a thorough materialism.

Santayana was often criticized for proposing an impossible leap in his theory of knowledge, jumping from a wholly immanent essence to an external object which stimulates the intuition of that essence. But here, at the very beginning of his inquiry, he leaps from an immaterial datum, supposedly all that we can be sure of, to an equal assurance of materialism. We are asked to accept two presuppositions, neither of which is self-evident, and which, taken together, are impossible to reconcile.

If, by Santayana's own description, an immaterial and immanent essence is "the bedrock of perfect certitude," and "I have absolute assurance of nothing save of some given essence" and "the rest is arbitrary belief" [32]—then how, in the name of consistency, let alone common sense, can I accept materialism as "the minimum presupposition of perception and action." [33]? I cannot even reach matter with any assurance or certitude, let alone embrace it as the almighty power and principle of the universe. Yet I am asked to accept materialism *a priori* as the ultimate principle of the universe and powerful producer of all things, including (inexplicably) this immaterial essence.

If Santayana is going to proceed "logically," as he promised, then he must profess a helpless idealism. To accept a real material world can be no more than "arbitrary belief." To accept materialism as the origin of the universe, and the exercise of all dynamic power, is not merely arbitrary but the most preposterous belief possible to him.

These irreconcilable and yet axiomatic presuppositions, of materialism as to the origin of the universe and symbolic subjectivism as to the origin of knowledge, precluded any sincere scepticism on Santayana's part. The basic method which Santayana used was not so much scepticism as transcendental criticism.

TRANSCENDENTAL CRITICISM

A reflexive criticism of knowledge is possible, but not by a radical transcendentalism which artificially separates the natural term of cognition. Both scepticism and transcendental criticism are futile methods by their very nature, since they attempt to criticize knowledge by implicitly denying it. There can be no criticism of knowledge without the very exercise of it, and what is self-evident is not merely a subjective appearance, a mere ghost of reality, but an existing object.

Transcendentalism initiates its inquiry with the gross assumption that the primitive datum of direct knowledge is a wholly subjective element: a phenomenon, an idea, or, in Santayana's case, an essence. But trans-subjective realism is certainly more in accord with common sense experience; its explanation is another and a psychological problem, impossible to solve on the basis of a materialistic metaphysic, as the proponents of Critical Neo-Realism discovered.

We cannot begin to subject cognition to critical analysis by destroying the nature of cognition in which there is an essential relation between the knowing subject and the object known. The nature of our cognitive powers is revealed in the exercise of those powers, and the act of cognition naturally terminates in a corresponding object.

The primitive object of direct knowledge cannot be the cognitive powers themselves, nor the Ego, but something other than the thinker. Etymologically, the very notion of object is "that which is thrown against": in this case something trans-subjective coming into contact with the knowing subject and stimulating awareness of it. The Ego is not known except through its experience of opposition to the datum. We have to move to one side, as it were, in order to look at the datum as such; and in this instance we are exercising indirect, reflexive knowledge. In direct knowledge we have an implicit self-knowledge which is attained only *in* the act or exercise of that knowledge, an act, furthermore, which terminates in an object in the sense of "something other."

Simply speaking, we know *something* before we know that we know. The first psychological stage of consciousness, contrary to Descartes, is not "I think" but "I know"—and this is not enough, for I must know *something*, in the sense that I know *something* is. Existence naturally precedes essence in our cognitive experience. Unwittingly or not, Santayana only reflects upon essence indirectly, in its apprehension or subjective state, in which it can be reconsidered as a logical character. The difficulty with transcendentalism is that it reverses the natural order of knowledge. Reflection does not begin the process of thought, nor thought begin the process of knowledge.

Certainly the case for realism is overwhelming and verified by common sense experience, not, however, in a crude materialistic form, nor on the basis of faith as a bridge out of complete subjectivism.

A proper critical method of examining our knowledge should be based upon the exigencies of the nature of thought, realized in the very exercise of knowledge. Reflecting, then, upon the true nature of thought, such a method can help it attain its natural end: the acquisition of truth by a union with extra-mental reality. A good critical method, accordingly, cannot be one which severs thought from its natural and necessary object.

Since an existing object is necessary to the exercise of human thought, any method is arbitrary, and doomed to failure, which, prior to a critical examination, assumes the absolute immanence of cognition and presupposes its transcendental character. This is the very question it proposes to answer and should be proffered, if at all, as a conclusion, not a presupposition.[34]

Every judgment is implicitly critical insofar as the mind perceives, in the very act of judgment, its natural conformity to things not itself. Judgment itself, however, can be criticized by another and explicit examination by reflecting upon the terms of judgment. This is a classical distinction, founded upon common sense experience, and enables us to distinguish between true judgment and a judgment of truth, discerning the formal and material elements of discourse.

The question of truth, and of immediate realism, must be considered again. Here we are concerned only with method; and the point to be made is that by employing introspection and, more pertinently, transcendentalism, Santayana assumes an artificial approach to the term of essence, inevitably leading to a distortion of its character into a curious and inconsistent hybrid. The result of his method is an immediate intuition of essence, not the simple apprehension of the quiddity of a material existent, but an altogether subjective concoction with neither foundation nor origin. And this is made possible only by presupposing the immanence of this essence, simply because the mind can consider it abstractly.

Although existence precedes essence in the order of knowledge, Santayana, in reflection, can deny existence to an essence by abstracting from its fundamental conditions. In positing essence as the sole datum of consciousness, he is deluded by his initial transcendence from the natural object of knowledge.

Essence, he concludes, without any necessary reference to existence, is all that is immediately evident to intuition. By what right can he make this claim? Certainly not on the basis of experience, but only by transcending existence speculatively. That we have immediate intuition through external sensation, in that objects are immediately present to us, and that we can apprehend abstracted essences in intellection is all very true; but that these "appearances," as Santayana loosely calls them, are purely subjective and not at all existent, is a gross assumption and surely not evident in experience.

Before any investigation, experience shows that we know extra-mental objects and do not intuit merely "specious" essences underived from these objects. And a valid cognitional critique, based on the nature of knowledge, can justify this postulate of common sense.

Santayana tells us he is "constrained merely to register as a brute fact the emergence of consciousness in animals" and yet a page later insists that "a pure and radical transcendentalism will disclaim all knowledge of fact." [35] Passing over this inconsistency, one among many, we can assert that the "shrewd orthodoxy" of experience registers as a brute fact, critically justified by a proper examination of our knowledge according to its nature, the direct contact of consciousness with extra-mental, existing reality. It is only on the basis of distorted introspection and transcendentalism that Santayana asserts otherwise. Transcendentalism is the trap of idealism, and once in its jaws there is no escape, even by leaps of faith.

It is unfortunate that Santayana did not make a better choice in his preference for *some* Greek philosophers. Curiously enough he accuses certain Greek philosophers (which probably means all but Democritus) of a lack of realism, saying: "They seldom or never reverted to the immediate for a foothold in thought. . . ." [36] Aristotelian philosophy is founded upon the immediate observation of physical nature, from which it induces principles and then deduces conclusions, and insists that the mind possesses nothing which does not have its foundation in sense experience. Santayana, on the other hand, founds his philosophy on sceptical and transcendental introspection, closing his eyes to the universe and examining a truncated version of being. In method he did not even return to the ancients; he never went beyond Descartes. And he has suffered a similar fate.[37]

CONCLUSION

"The introspection into which I may ultimately plunge, when I seem to be creating the world when I think it, is a violently artificial exercise, in which the wheels of life are reversed. . . ." [38] This is not a critic's judgment on Santayana's method; it is his own judgment leveled against idealism. While he inveighed against ultimate idealism which would create the world out of discourse, his own transcendental introspection forced him into the same subjectivism with only a weak cry of faith to posit a world at all.

"They," he says of the idealists, "retract the primary presuppositions of intelligence implied in their own arguments." [39] This is precisely what Santayana himself has done in his rejection of the first principles of thought and being, the basic foundation of any sane philosophy. His scepticism affords him nothing, except to pose as a purified thinker, starting afresh, when actually he works from the gratuitous and irreconcilable presuppositions of materialism and radical transcendentalism. Pouncing upon a truncated datum and calling it essence, he proposes it as an immediate and self-evident intuition, with a wholly subjective character—an enormous presumption, contrary to the common sense experience to which he professed to adhere.

In the end, he admitted the barrenness of this truncated term, the fresh fruit of transcendentalism: "only some random essence, staring and groundless;" then came the irrational declaration that all knowledge is belief; he thereupon decided what was to be believed. He hoped he had posited

afresh "the notions of substance, soul, nature, and discourse
. . . with my eyes open." And he criticized the dogmas of
others as "incoherent and incapable of serving as the basis of
any reasonable system." [40]

At least this much is certain: he did indeed posit afresh the
notions of substance, soul, nature, and discourse,—but only
by closing his eyes to their existence. And it is amusing to
find him condemning the dogmas of others as incoherent and
incapable of serving as the basis of any reasonable system,
when he himself denied reason's essential relation to existing
reality, and called existence "necessarily irrational and inexplicable." [41]

He failed to mention that he has also posited afresh the
notion of essence. We shall note it for him.

Chapter Two

Term

LET us recall and clarify the origin of essence in the mind of Santayana. He began his philosophical inquiry with an impure and short-lived scepticism. This becomes evident immediately with his presumption of the immanence of knowledge—the Kantian transcendental critique which is a begging of the question proposed, since it decides upon the nature of knowledge before investigating it.[1]

Santayana expresses this presumption by declaring against any immediate apprehension of things "outside" which imply "external" or "adventitious" relations. He protests that "belief in the existence of anything . . . is something radically incapable of proof" because it rests "on some irrational persuasion of life."[2] This proposition involves a denial of reasoning about the existence of things absent (Robinson Crusoe, therefore, was "irrational" to induce the presence of another inhabitant on his island from his discovery of fresh footprints); and a presumption that existents immediately present are not self-evident (the fact that they are so does away with both the possibility and necessity of direct proof).

"Essence," he decides, "is the least ultimate term in scepticism. . . ."[3] This term is the "bed-rock of certitude . . . somewhat discouragingly it turns out to be in the regions of the rarest ether. I have absolute assurance of nothing save of the character of some given essence. The rest is arbitrary belief or interpretation added by my animal impulse." And he concludes this decision by saying: "I am resigned to being a dogmatist; but at what point shall my dogmatism begin, and by what first solicitation of nature?" [4]

This last question which he asks himself is anticlimatic. His dogmatism has been exercised already. His first solicitation of nature has been an assumption of nature's self-sufficiency and a dissection of the nature of knowledge; and he has most decisively abandoned his pretended scepticism by declaring that the datum, an essence, without implicit consignification of existence, is the bedrock of certitude, alone giving absolute assurance.

This ambitious opinion can be challenged, both on the grounds of common sense experience and a critical examination of that experience in cognition.

Why does Santayana decide upon an intuition of essence, entirely divested of existence even implicitly given? Because "existence is a conjunction of natures in adventitious and variable relations" and "according to this definition, it is evident that existence can never be given in intuition. . . ." [5] Here Santayana also "posits afresh" the notion of existence. Like every introspective philosopher, excogitating a system transcendentally, he presumes a starting point, makes his own definitions, and then, as consistently as he can, elaborates and develops the implications of these definitions. As Santayana observes, and indeed it is the wisest observation that he makes, ". . . everything turns on the meaning of *existence*. . . ." [6]

To Be or Not To Be

Hamlet's dilemma turns on existence, and no one questions the meaning of this passage of his soliloquy. He is not wondering whether it is better to be the harassed Prince of Denmark or a less troubled peasant in the fields beyond the castle walls. His personal identity is not at stake. The question is whether or not existence, considering his manifold difficulties in the actual experience of it, is better than death, the severance of the mortal coil that binds him to earthly existence. Hamlet's question is a profound metaphysical problem as well. For the question is one of *being:* the very object of metaphysics and a crucial point in Santayana's development of his doctrine of essence.

Santayana disclaimed any pretense to metaphysics. Yet he plunges into it with a vengeance, raising his philosophy on a metaphysical term, essence, and proceeding to analyze pure being, non-being, possible being, universals, eternal and infinite entities, etc. He believes that he avoids the currently opprobrious name of metaphysician merely because he clings to materialism and uses Platonic notions without "hypostasizing" them. Materialism, however, insofar as it seeks to explain all things through an ultimate, originative, creative matter, is a metaphysic. And Santayana followed Plato further than he realized; in fact, he has overtaken him and gone beyond.

A philosopher cannot avoid, at least implicitly, working from some notion of being; and whatever that notion may be it will determine the rest of his philosophy. Santayana founds his philosophy on being (or we might say "half-being") and treats it explicity when he indicates his own meaning of the word *is.*[7]

To return to Hamlet, we know that a solution to his dilemma was forced upon him. After his tragic demise, it could be said appropriately: "Hamlet is no more." Obviously, in such a proposition, the signification is that Hamlet no longer exists in this world and has shuffled off the mortal coil. The meaning is not that Hamlet is no longer Prince of Denmark; this is true, but only because he no longer exists in order to be either prince or pauper.

The primary meaning of the copula *is* is not an indication

of a subject or a predicate; *is* contains the meaning of existence in itself. The verb *is* signifies existence and does so in its own right. All judgments of adjectival attribution, moreover, are expressed through the copula *is* (e.g. Hamlet is demented), because these attributive judgments mean to say *how* a certain thing actually *is*. That a thing *is* precedes any mode or condition of its existence. A proper understanding of logic and grammar, and their relationship, makes this clear enough. Existence is enacted before it is signified, and therefore implicit, or consignified, even in the apprehension of a thing before a judgment is made concerning its existence.

Santayana, on the other hand, says that "of all the meanings of the word *is*—existence, substance, equivalence, definition, etc., the most radical and proper is that in which I may say of anything that it is what it is." [8] To be, therefore, in the meaning he assigns to it, is not equated with existence but indicative only of essential self-identity. The metaphysics thickens; for now we come to the crucial notion of being. What does being mean to Santayana, and how does his notion of being affect his philosophy?

BEING AND ESSENCE

We can approach being in our study of it as we do naturally and directly in our experience of it: by recognizing being as it first comes to the intellect abstracted from a concrete object. [9] Instead, let us back into this notion with Santayana via deliberated scepticism and pseudo-criticism.

When all preferred denials are made and the sceptic retreats to his artificial solipsism (artificial because it is based on an unreal transcendence of the natural object of knowledge), where has he arrived? He has come to the "important conclusion" that the datum—a discovered essence—"does not exist." Santayana has jolted his critics with this proposition.

But the conclusion need not be shocking at all. Although important, it is not remarkable; for, properly understood, the statement is true.

Essence does not, indeed cannot, really exist apart from the act of existence. For together they are entitative parts of every real being. Although these co-principles are really distinct in all creatures, they are not and cannot be separated but only distinguished. But, because they can be distinguished intellectually, an even bolder assertion can be made by saying that existence does not exist, an observation made nearly 500 years ago by Cardinal Cajetan, St. Thomas's principal commentator. He pointed out that existence is exercised as a principle of real being and signified in the apprehension of a quiddity; and this signification can be considered logically as a distinguishable something.[10]

Actually, although really distinct in contingent beings, essence and existence in real being are not separable since they unite to make being *be*. Even an abstracted essence merely takes on a new (intentional) mode of existence in the intellect, without losing its physical existence in the substance from which it is drawn and always signifying it. Being is what comes first to the mind and always remains. The mind can focus on essence, obscuring its relation to existence, but cannot abstract existence from essence, since existence is not a form but the act of all forms.

True enough, "everything turns on the meaning of existence," more precisely on the meaning of being, since existence is the primary and inalienable principle of being. Being is *that which is;* or, simply and affirmatively, *what is:* a two-term expression but indicative of a single substance. The mind necessarily apprehends being by abstraction, initially through the sensation of concrete objects. We become aware of a *whatness* and an *isness*, and may be tempted to consider them apart. The danger arises if we shift the emphasis from the *is* to the *what*. Then an abstracted essence may seem ground-less, and appear, as it does for Santayana, "irrelevant" to existence.

By artificially considering existence apart from essence, knowledge becomes for Santayana, as he is fond of saying, "a salute, not an embrace." On the contrary, cognitive experience, and a proper critical analysis of that experience, reveals knowledge to be a union of the most intimate nature possible: an identity of intellect with its object without either one losing its own proper unity, so that Aristotle, speaking of the intellect's grasp of being, can say that, in a sense, the soul is all things. Unfortunately, Santayana leaned more on Plato than on Aristotle.

SANTAYANA'S PLATONIC HERITAGE

In his reading of the Greek philosophers, Santayana was attracted to the materialism of Democritus and the idealism of Plato. There is no real opposition between these two philosophical directions; for there is a latent idealism in every materialist.[11] Essentialism leaves a philosopher metaphysically limping, unable to account for existence and the necessity and eternity of essences themselves; and the problems that plagued Plato had to be faced, or ignored, by Santayana. While many of his predecessors, Leibniz and Hegel most prominently among them, contributed to Santayana's doctrine of essence, it is to Plato that he is indebted more than any other philosopher.

Plato's ουσια reverberates throughout Santayana's doctrine of essence. This notion, sometimes translated "the really real," can be called "essence" insofar as it points to that quality which gives it eminent reality: sameness or self-identity.[12] Passages from Plato's *Timaeus* and *Phaedo* on this attribute of identity are almost verbally identical with Santayana's descriptions.

Plato found himself in difficulties explaining the precise reality of being restricted to self-identity; Santayana fares no better. For if being is sameness, non-being is otherness, and every being participates in non-being insofar as this essence is no other essence. Santayana states his position in just this manner.[13] Sameness can never account for reality as long as being is equated with essential self-identity. M. Gilson considers this classical Platonic circle:

> Nothing can be that which it is, without, at the same time, not being that which it is not. Moreover, each being is the same as itself only, whereas, it is other than all the rest. It is therefore the same but once, whereas it is "other" as many times as there are other things. Now, since to be is to be the same, and since to be other is not to be, any given thing can be called a being but once, against the infinite number of times when it must be said not to be. In short, according to the number of other beings that there are, so many times is it true to say that a given being is not, although, in respect of its own selfhood, this one being alone is, while all the other ones are not.[14]

There is a similar difficulty in accounting for mutual relations: any single essence stands in opposing relations to anything not itself and consequently entails a multiplicity of relations while remaining itself and never revealing in itself the cause of its relations. A principle must be found to account for the internal consistency of an essence, along with the mutual compatibility of its relations. Whence comes the eternal verity of an essence? Since Santayana denies that essences are abstracted from things, how do they arise in intuition at all and how do they assume "external relations" when "incarnated"? He ignores these problems, for the most part, except to refer to a "dark principle" (dark indeed!).[15]

He is content to let the potentiality of matter somehow and "irrationally" create its own form.

There is no legitimate exit from his essence; yet we are asked to accept a self-explanatory nature, matter "budding" its own immaterial essences; and if essences are intuited they are "kindled by fancy," apparently an immaterial function "emerging" from the material. We are, let it be remembered, supposed to be philosophizing on the basis of common sense. Plato recognized the necessity of reaching higher than essence to account for anything, including essence itself.[16] Santayana, however, never gets beyond a diaphanous "pure Being," which M. Maritain justly calls *pseudo-being*, because it is purely logical. Although originating in the experienced knowledge of real being, it is divorced from reality through transcendentalism and becomes a ghostly reflection.[17]

Mr. Cory, Santayana's disciple, says that he called Santayana's attention to Whitehead's proposal of a necessary divine "conceptual envisagement" to explain the determination of essence in the actual order of the universe. Santayana's reply is quoted by Cory: [18]

> "What does Whitehead mean by a 'conceptual envisagement' of the realm of essence? In order to 'envisage,' that is to *face* anything, there must first be the psyche—an animal body which by its reaction in a natural medium gives birth to spirit and a perspective of the world."

This incredible response, in which "conceptual envisagement" is understood literally and univocally,[19] apparently satisfied Cory, who blandly stated that the difference between Santayana and Whitehead on this critical point was merely a "matter of temperament." Assuredly, there is some element of temperament in this answer of Santayana's, considering his stubborn recurrence to the great axiom of materialism and his absorption with imagery to the exclusion of reality. The latter tendency is evident in nearly all his references to religion, in which he sees nothing but its imaginative expression. For example, he makes the astonishing statement: "That God is a spirit, though the text be orthodox, has never been the popular belief, nor have theologians taken it seriously." [20] The last place where Santayana will found his essences is in God. Plato's proposal of subsisting essences arose from his isolation of essence apart from their necessary existential setting; and Santayana only ignores the Platonic problem by relegating his essences at last into an ideal nothingness. The actual must be postulated as self-explanatory.

TRUNCATED BEING

Santayana's metaphysical error, a consequence of his transcendentalism, is to confuse essence with being, a mistake which is understandable because of the fact that essence can be considered abstractly. By stopping at simple apprehension, which is incomplete knowledge preparatory to a judgment of existence as exercized, he has taken essence from its conceptual setting where it has intentional existence as signified, and makes a pseudo-reality of it. Again, M. Gilson, very much to the point:

> The most serious mistake made by the various metaphysics of essence is their failure to realize the nature of essence. They simply forget that essence always is the essence of some being. . . . The primary error of the metaphysics of essence is to mistake a part for its whole and to speculate about essences as though they were the whole of both reality and its intelligibility. . . . I may well abstract the essence of a certain being and deal with it for a while as though it were unrelated to the being from which I abstracted it, but it is not, for *essentia* always belongs to an *esse*, and even while I conceive it apart, essence never cuts loose from actual being; it is, rather, bound to it by a life line, and, if that line is cut off, essence is dead. No knowledge will ever come out of it.[21]

This sums up Santayana's position exactly, since he does conclude explicitly to "inert" essences. He pretends to absolutely no knowledge proceeding from them; yet, in philosophizing, he treats them extensively as objects of knowledge. And while he resorts to a pledge of "animal faith" as a means of knowledge, this blind, groping instinct makes the preposterous claim of evident materialism as to the existence of those things which it cannot even reach intellectually, including its own immaterial spirit which is the only initial self-evident reality!

Abstraction

Santayana does not admit abstraction of essences from things, because he initially decided upon the absolute immanence of essences. In one instance he talks around the problem, pointing out the obvious fact that essence, a *term*, cannot be identified with the *act* of abstraction.[22] Elsewhere he denies that his essences are abstract terms because "there is no other datum, more individual or more obvious, from which the abstraction could be drawn." [23] But this merely brings us back to his original presumption of transcendentalism that the immanent alone is more evident than a trans-subjective object, and implies that indirect knowledge is more direct than direct knowledge. Furthermore, by concrete example, this postulate would imply that "red" (which does not exist alone and can be considered only logically and reflexively as a quality) is *more individual* than a particular red object.

This matter of abstraction must be considered again in treating Santayana's essences in their cognitional function; here it suffices to point out that in practice Santayana can't avoid speaking of essences in terms denoting abstraction from existing things: (Italics mine)

In other words, in order to reach the intuition of pure Being, *it is requisite to rise altogether above the sense of existence.* [RB (E) 47]

When *clarified* and thoroughly actualized, all data are essences. . . . [RB (T) 438]

The datum of intuition, when fully *realized and clarified,* reveals nothing but itself to that intuition. It is an essence. . . . [RB (S) 649]

More explicitly:

An essence is an idea, but *an idea lifted out of its immersion in existing objects* and in existing feelings. . . . ["Apologia Pro Mente Sua," 500]

When *abstracted from our own presence and interests,* everything that can be found or imagined is reduced to a mere essence. . . . ["Carnival" in *Soliloquies in England,* 140]

In these quotations it should be noted that not only one but two abstractions are made in order to reach that point where essences become "logical characters." From the sensation of external objects, immediately existing and present, Santayana abstracts an idea; then he reconsiders the idea as a logical quiddity. A grotesque logicalization of logic results. This is the result of attempting to consider essence separated from existence.

"All real essences," as M. Gilson points out, "are known through abstraction. Yet their abstraction does not entail their separation from existence. Such a separation never occurs until essentialism begins to deal with them as abstractions from abstractions. Essences then become *entia tertiae intentionis,* and they are dead." [24]

TELEOLOGY AND TRUTH

Let us turn, very briefly, to teleology and truth in this confusing essentialism. The denial of causality, while employing it implicitly and explicitly in practice,[25] does not deserve consideration. Everything becomes reversed for Santayana: matter determines form and, teleologically, organs determine functions.[26]

Santayana, supposedly founding his philosophy on common sense, and backtracking to a transcendental essentialism which should be mute as to knowledge, dares to tell us it is "absurd to imagine that the shape taken by things [in nature] was an aim pursued in their taking it." [27]

On the contrary, if we reason (rather than imagine), considering the actuality of things, it is clear that there must be definite and discernible principles influencing any existing being. Otherwise we would be unable to distinguish being from non-being, nor would one particular being be distinguishable from another. Why should one thing be such as it is, rather than something else? It would not be anything at all unless determined to *be something*. To the discerning intellect, not only is final cause evident but also a formal cause determined by a selected purpose, and an efficient cause making that selection and imposing the determined form upon the potentiality of matter. In his consideration of causality, Santayana is befogged by his imagination so that he cannot perceive realities beyond the language that serves as signs of concepts, which in turn are those very realities apprehended by the intellect. Nor can he conceive the notion of a formal cause without ascribing to it the act of an efficient cause.[28]

As for truth, we are interested, at this point, in Santayana's reference of truth to being. Truth, he understands, ontologically and comprehensively: ". . . the complete ideal description of existence. . . ." [29]—". . . what omniscience would assert, the whole ideal system of qualities and relations which the world has exemplified or will exemplify." [30] All things, as he says, seen under the form of eternity—but without anyone seeing them, for truth also is "something in the realm of essence." [31] Truth, then, is not convertible with being, insofar as existing things are related to an intellect measuring or measured by them; truth is convertible with essences exemplified, but abstractly considered by no one: another abstraction from abstraction.

Furthermore, "there are no necessary truths," only "logical consistency." [32] Why? Because "truth being descriptive of existence, and existence being contingent, truth will be contingent also." [33] Once again the separation of essence from existence is apparent.

For while it is true to say that any composite being, subject to generation and corruption, is contingent in its coming and going; nevertheless, *while it exists it necessarily exists and necessarily is that which it is.* "The whole is greater than any of its parts" is a necessary truth, not that the dead concept of "whole," reconsidered by a double abstraction, is more of a mental content than "part"—but that the whole of any determined thing is more than any part of it: a necessary truth grasped by the intellect by an abstraction of the proposition as gleaned from the sense experience of an existing whole in relation to its parts. Logical truth is the intellect's equation with being, with that which really is, and not a merely consistent pattern of logical terms.

DEFINITIONS AND DISTINCTIONS

We have assumed, from previous examination, that Santayana's notion of essence is that of a quiddity, reviewed by additional logical speculation; so that the resultant term is not the essence of an existing thing, reviewed by a second intention of the mind focusing on this abstraction, but re-reviewed without reference to existence of any kind: "irrelevant," as Santayana often says, to existence. This term is the effect of a divisive transcendentalism that cuts essences away from their roots in existence and tosses them into the ever-receding reflections of speculation until they become "inert" and mere "ghosts"—*entia tertiae intentionis*.

To pin down Santayana's notion of essence is not an easy task. His fluent and florid prose, his fluctuating definitions, his sudden leaps of thought and quick changes of supposition, preclude clarity or consistency.

Indications of this confusion: essences are not possible being [RB (E), pp. 26-27], yet they are "primordial and distinct forms of possible being" [RB (T), p. 430]; the datum (essence) is "an image" [S-AF, p. 34]; but not "the imaginary" [RB (E), p. 29]; the datum is "an idea" [S-AF, p. 35], and yet "it is not an idea" [RB (E), p. 41]. We do not know essences, only objects and events [S-AF, p. 169]; however "to know surprise by experience is the only way of knowing its essence" [S-AF, p. 276]. "Spirit is a category, not an individual being" [S-AF, p. 275]. Yet an individual's experience is "spirit thinking" [S-AF, p. 204]. "All data and descriptions are equally essences, terms of human discourse" [S-AF, p. 204]; but essences are not to be confused with language [RB (E), p. 41]. By memory we identify past with present intuition [S-AF, p. 151]; we cannot, however, identify one essence with another because "the identity of an essence with itself is absolute" [RB (E), p. 37].

A recital of these confusions and apparent contradictions is not made for the sake of embarrassing the philosopher, but only to indicate the inconsistencies encountered and their origin. They arise not only from a lack of precision in expression but, more basically, from a lack of sufficient discrimination and distinction of entities.[34]

A special instance of a disturbing lack of distinction occurs in the confusion of essence with form. "The flux of nature," he says, "could not be a flux, nor at all perceptible, unless it was a flux through essences, that is, through forms of being differing from one another." [35] Essence is also described as "any actual aspect which anything can wear, determining its nature, or revealing it to an attentive mind." [36]

Mr. Cory, the faithful disciple, desiring to eschew "words of the trade," attempts to explain essence by citing a personal experience of it. He observes the sky change its color from crimson to gray, bewails the event of this lovely crimson changing to drab gray, then on reflection realizes that crimson cannot change to anything other than it is. He concludes: "It is not the *essences* of things that grow, alter, or are subject to decay, but the pulses and congeries of existence that borrow these qualities. . . ." [37]

Cory, in narrating this experience, offers a good instance of qualitative change. Dropping the picturesque phrasing ("pulses and congeries"), we can say, with more technical precision, that the subject of change is a substance: in this instance, the cloud vapors which have refracted colored sunlight and impinged it upon the retina of the eye. The substance involved is water in the form of moisture. The accidental quality of color, so easily gained and lost, is an essence only in a secondary and relative sense, since its being is wholly dependent upon the substance in which it adheres —merely *ens entis*, as it is appropriately called by Aristotle. Crimson, as such, has no absolute essence; for it has no being except to be *in* the substance which it qualifies and by which it is supported. Accidents live on borrowed essences and existences, and in the natural order of things, apart from some substance, they are dead—as are all qualities in Santayana's graveyard of essences.

The point is that precise definitions and distinctions are necessary for us to distinguish the manifold elements that enter into our consideration of composite and complex substances. Considering the nature of the universe and the nature of our knowledge of it, we must pick our way carefully. Normally we do not have an intuition of being, since the recognition of being as exercised comes with judgment, by which we compose and divide apprehended concepts, predicating their existence or non-existence.

Santayana has wielded his own razor, first cutting existence away from essence and, secondly, shaving away numerous distinctions necessary to man's understanding of reality as he approaches the natural object of his intellect: the quiddities of sensible being. Scholastic philosophers speculated more naturally and more precisely, putting first things first as they appear to the inquiring mind and making proper distinctions.[38]

The being first apprehended by the mind is real being, not a logical entity resulting from a review of the primitive datum. St. Thomas points out that existence precedes essence logically, in that the mind grasps the notion of essence by its apprehension of the essence of some existing thing.[39] We cannot, strictly speaking, abstract existence from the essence grasped, for existence is not a form but the act of all forms, and is necessarily consignified even in the simple apprehension of essence.

In this apprehension the essence does not lose its existence; in fact it cannot; it merely takes on a new status of existence, intentional existence, in the mind, and real existence is thereby signified. We can refer back to this intentional existence by a second consideration of the mind; but to ignore existence altogether is, while possible, an altogether artificial, mental side-stepping, which achieves not the being of second intention, proper to logic, but a being of third intention, a chimera, indeed "ghostly" and "inert" because it is dead—this is Santayana's notion of essence.

Conclusion

Santayana was impatient of logic and its formidable demonstrations; but he would have profited by pondering this neat syllogism, proposed by the learned Cardinal Cajetan:

Everyone who makes mistakes about the principles of intelligible being will err more concerning other matters.

Everyone who makes mistakes about essence and being errs in the matter of first principles of intelligible being.

Therefore, everyone making mistakes in dealing with essence and being will err more in other matters.[40]

Chapter Three

Function

AN ANALYSIS of Santayana's notion of essence exposes three functions or operations of essence: (a) essences make change and multiplicity possible, enabling the flux of existence to be a flux at all; (b) specious essences (those intuited) serve as symbols of both subjective states and objects of knowledge, becoming definable in terms, which also are essences; [1] (c) they have moral or aesthetic value as objects of contemplation.

ESSENCES IN NATURE

We have already considered the problem of essences realized in nature, relevant to the difficulty of deriving multiplicity from the notion of being as self-identity and with regard to manifestations of a teleological direction in nature. Santayana must rely on "a dark principle" and a "balance of tensions" to account for diversity and unity in species and the apparent regularity of the universe. The great axiom of materialism must be accepted on faith, and we are asked to consider all order and regularity as multiple and diverse spontaneous happenings.

Santayana is weighted down by the heavy handicap of materialism, which cannot be defended reasonably. The axiom of materialism, of self-sufficient nature, must be accepted as a "minimum presupposition," even though it is entirely irreconcilable with a transcendentalism which proposes an immaterial essence as the only certitude. Why do definite forms of things appear, with observable regularity and apparent teleological direction? They just do. There is no explanation. We must register another "brute fact."

If, as Santayana protests, matter cannot be restricted to any philosopher's notion of it (even granting for the moment his symbolic nominalism, and passing over the fact of our natural knowledge of what things are by observing what they do)—then how can he have any assurance, to the point of making an axiom, of his own idea of matter as self-explanatory, creative, omnipotent, etc., being a true representation of the reality of matter? [2] He is convicted out of his own mouth through his own principles.

Matter, by its observable potentiality, can not in the same instance of generation be actuality; nor can the material, of itself, ever account for the immaterial. "It is astounding," exclaims a popular historian of philosophy, "that so subtle a thinker and so ethereal a poet as Santayana should tie to his neck the millstone of a philosophy which after centuries of effort is as helpless as ever to explain the growth of a flower or the laughter of a child." [3]

ESSENCE IN KNOWLEDGE

Santayana says that essences "are indispensable terms in the perception of matters of fact, and *render transitive knowledge possible*." [4] The italics are mine, for this point is important: first, because the notion of essence was supposed to supply the medium in transitive knowledge, according to the Critical Neo-Realists who were opposing both idealism and the materialistic copyism of the naive realists; secondly, because the fate of essence hangs on its relation to cognition, since its appearance must, in some way, be dependent on an external object.

Now Santayana began to philosophize with the presumption that the datum is an essence, wholly immanent and "irrelevant" to existents. Granting the presumed premise, how does this specious essence arise at all and how can it have any relation to an object that is material and, according to Santayana, "outside"?

"The stimulus," he says, "that calls animal attention to some external fact, in provoking an act of the body, also presents some image to the mind." [5] Essences, however, are nowhere, for they do not exist. "You cannot go in search of that which is nowhere. Some essences will appear or occur to you, since whatever intuition life may awaken in you must light up some essence or the other." [6] But what elicits this appearance of an essence? We are told that "intuition arises when the inner life of the animal, or its contact with external things, is expressed in some actual appearance, in some essence given in feeling or thought." [7] Some disturbance, then, internal or external, occasions the intuition. But these are occasions, not causes. If essences are nowhere, how do they come to be somewhere: namely, in intuition? Is there a selective agent stretching an invisible hand into nowhere and choosing a particular, immaterial essence for spirit to intuit?

First, Santayana tells us "the psyche and the material circumstances . . . determine the choice and succession of themes on which intuition shall be employed in some particular person. . . ." [8] Twenty-one pages later we read that essences are not "selected or produced by any living soul, [since they are] inert, infinite and latent." [9] We are moved back into the darkness again. And material circumstances can hardly determine a specious essence with which it has no contact.

Santayana gives an example: if "some material thing called a triangle is placed before me at a suitable distance, my eyes and brain will do the rest, and the essence dear to Euclid will arise in my mind's eye." [10] What is the function of the eyes if all qualities perceived arise solely from an internal impulse? And why does *this* essence dear to Euclid arise rather than another: a square or a circle or parallel lines?

At one point we think we will have an answer. "But whence," the philosopher asks himself, "the choice of essences that shall appear in intuition? How does the psyche arrive at any of these creatures rather than at any other?" [11] Here we should have an answer. But it is not forthcoming. Instead we are told that the psyche doesn't gather them out of her substance or the tropes she imposes on her own matter. Then we are informed that essences (now understood as the perceptible qualities of things) are not in the things in which they appear. That position is "unfortunately untenable." No, in the tradition of Locke, all these qualities are subjective. It is more tenable, supposedly, to hold that colors, sounds, shapes—all sensations—are purely internal. But why does *this* color or *this* sound appear rather than others, if they are purely subjective in origin? No answer is given.

So far, we are entirely closeted in a blind subjectivism by which certain "essences" appear. They just do, another brute fact. This is the first blind leap, altogether unreasonable since no reason is given or, for that matter, possible.

Now how does this essence of such very mysterious origin have any relevance to an external object? We posit the "hidden object" beyond intuition by intent through "animal presumption, positing whatever object instinct is materially disposed to cope with, as in hunger, love, fighting, or the expectation of a future." [12] Accordingly, it seems that if I am hungry I intend a loaf of bread and there it is, and the same for the object of my affections, the enemy I wish to attack, and the overdue bus I am expecting.

"But how," a critic has justifiably asked, "does mental reference of ideas to things establish the external existence of things? . . . Since essences are developed independently of existences, why are existences implied in them?" [13] Undoubtedly Santayana would reply that existences do not depend on our idea of them. True enough, but utterly unverifiable by Santayana's transcendentalism, a trap from which he never escapes through a reasonable release.

So now we have two leaps. And this he admits: "Transitiveness in knowledge has two stages or leaps: the leap of intuition, from the state of the living organism to the consciousness of some essence; and the leap of faith or action, from the symbol actually given in sense or in thought to some ulterior existing object." [14] Surely these are very arbitrary and unreasonable leaps, with no motivations grounded in common sense to take them at all.

Santayana assures us that "Any given essence is normally a true sign for the object or event which occupies animal attention when that essence appears." [15] But what kind of sign is an essence? Purely arbitrary, since they are frequently called "terms of discourse;" there is no common quality between the sign and what is signified; for there is no reference to existence contained in an essence.

In the very beginning of his philosophical investigation, he had said that after pushing scepticism as far as it would go, he hoped to show that: "intelligence is veridical and that its ambition to reach the truth is sane and capable of satisfaction, even if each of its efforts actually fails." [16] This is a strange manifestation of confidence in the ability of the intellect to reach truth, for he calls truth an "ideal description of existence," and by his transcendentalism he cuts existence away from the intellect and claims it has no direct contact with existence!

Has the intellect an indirect contact between essences embodied in nature and those given in intuition, so that a comparison can be made? Apparently, for he says that "This complex or series of forms in the universe compose the truth about it; and this is the side of reality approachable by the intellect." [17] Furthermore, "if any mind is to perceive that flux [i.e., existence], or to distinguish any of its phases, it cannot do so otherwise than by discerning some essence exemplified there, which limits one phase or one moment and divides it from another." [18]

But how, may we ask, can we discern any essence in flux when, as he says, "the essences embodied in the depths and unattainable dimensions of nature escape us altogether," [19]— and—"nothing accurate can be said of a thing supposed to bridge two moments of time"? [20] There can be no comparison between the essences of things, changing from moment to moment, and the essences given in intuition. Furthermore, he insists that "knowledge can never lie in an overt comparison between one datum with another." [21] How then can the intellect be said to be veridical? How is any truth ever to be known?

Santayana asks the crucial question but never answers it: "If we ask how it happens that quite fresh essences, spontaneously evoked in intuition . . . can nevertheless apply to nature, the answer is not far to seek. Ideas apply to their occasions because they arise out of them, and are a part of the total natural event which controls their development." [22] But this reply does not answer the question asked; for we have not been told *how* ideas arise out of these occasions, nor how the intuited essence can have any real reference to nature.

The Fate of Discourse and Science

Any discourse whatsoever becomes an apparent impossibility since, according to Santayana, "it is impossible to arrest two intuitions and compare their objects" [23] and "the mind . . . cannot know that this essence is the one intended, possessed elsewhere by an intuition numerically different and historically remote." [24] I have already noted that with the comprehensive sense that Santayana gives to essence, he must and does admit that: "It is not likely that the same essence should ever appear twice in human experience." [25] This being so, then the very notion of essence is itself an essence (a "term of discourse"), so that as Santayana repeatedly reflects on this notion he must always find something different. Hence he cannot even claim logical consistency in his lengthy discourse on essence.

There can be no assignable reason for the experienced intelligibility of any discourse, according to Santayana's principles. He says that all discourse has "an arbitrary starting point and an arbitrary direction of progress. It picks up this essence or that for no reason that it can assign. . . . The fact that this essence rather than any other is being considered is a brute fact; and my discourse as a whole is sheer accident, initiated, if initiated at all, by some ambushed power." [26] Once again, driven by his original postulates into an inexplicable and unreasonable position, Santayana must register a "brute fact"—the only answer given to our question as to the selectivity of essence. That consciousness emerges in animal bodies is a brute fact; that one essence rather than another rises in intuition is also a brute fact. It is unfortunate that Santayana did not notice more evident brute facts in the early stages of his inquiries.

If discourse is hopeless, can we turn to the scientists work-

ing silently with their instruments to help us to the knowledge of physical objects? We might think so when Santayana tells us: "It is for science and further investigation of
the object to pronounce on the truth of our belief. . . ." [27]
What of the symbols "irrelevant to existence" with which
they are compelled to express their investigations? He replies
elsewhere: "I rely on them [the scientists] to discover gradually exactly which elements in their description of nature
may be literally true, and which merely symbolical: even
if they were all symbolical they would be true enough for
me. . . ." [28]

They must, of course, following Santayana's principles, be
all symbolical; and even if they were not, by what criterion
could we distinguish the literal from the symbolical? Santayana expresses himself more consistently elsewhere:

> The discouragement we may feel in science does not come
> from failure; it comes from a false conception of what would
> be success. Our worst difficulties arise from the assumption
> that knowledge of existences ought to be literal, whereas
> knowledge of existences has no need, no propensity, and no
> fitness to be literal. It is symbolic initially and . . . remains
> symbolic to the end. Can anything be more evident than that
> religion, language, patriotism, love, science itself speak in
> symbols? [29]

DIRECTIONS TOWARDS A SOLUTION

What is more evident is that language may be either literal
or metaphorical; it is not at all evident that all language is
metaphorical, nor that all literal terms are univocal. For Santayana, not only are words arbitrary symbols but also concepts, since they express arbitrary essences equally symbolic.
The difficulty arises from his notion that an idea, in order to
be proposed as true, must be a total comprehension. [30] This

accounts for his refusal to accept abstraction as the basis of intellectual knowledge.

But man cannot comprehend the whole of reality, which is a divine prerogative, nor even the whole reality of any individual thing in its complex concretization. He can, however, reach the reality of a thing by his abstraction of essences from material substances which may provide him with an essential definition, but not the totally comprehensive and exhaustive quiddity. Santayana would have man either a pure spirit, with an angelic or even divine intellect, or reduce him to the incongruity of a dreaming vegetable.

Language is arbitrary, but significant as a communication of like concepts commonly obtained by men. Otherwise, all our talk would be unintelligible babbling. A difference of language does not affect the sameness of meaning intended. "Blue" and "azul" signify the identical reality apprehended by diverse peoples in different lands.[31]

Immediate contact with existence is also more evident than a merely subjective symbol arising from nowhere. "Intuition is born smothered in intent . . . turned towards the not-given,"[32] precisely because existence *is* given in immediate sense perception and signified in the simple apprehension of the intellect.[33]

When Miss Calkins, embroiled in the epistemological controversy raised by the Neo-Realists and Critical Neo-Realists, asked ". . . how can the qualities or the nature of a thing be detached from it. . . . ?"[34] she posed the proper question. That we do know qualities and natures in some direct manner is evident, but how we do is another and a psychological question. An examination would prove that they are immediately present intentionally, not physically; through a representative medium, but directly and not indirectly or symbolically.

We cannot offer a detailed response here, but only indicate the essential notes.

The proper objects of external sensation are immediately present, without requiring an image produced subjectively by the fancy. The image impressed immediately by a sense object present, as in the case of a retinal image, enables us, for example, to see the object and not the retinal image. That our external senses are intuitive of their proper objects is evident from experience and from the fact that we do distinguish reality from dreams and illusions.[35] If we do not know some things directly and in themselves, we can never verify any of our knowledge.[36]

Only accidentally, or in the case of common sensibles (size, shape, distance, etc.), does error arise in external sensation. Temperature is not the specific object of touch; and when Santayana resurrects the old problem of the hot hand in cold water or vice versa, he fails to notice that he does feel the touch of a liquid surface, which is all that the sense of touch is held to report. Water does have a determinable temperature when accidental interferences are not present; so does the human body.

In intellectual knowledge, acquired by abstracting the quiddities of individual sensible objects, the intellect, according to its immaterial but potential status, produces its own term as a medium by which the forms of things are united to itself. But this ideal similitude or species, an epistemological principle, is by nature intentional: its function being to yield knowledge directly of that which it represents. Thus an external object acquires an intentional existence in the mind, through which the object itself is known. Our knowledge is immediate in that ideas are not directly *what* we know, but that *by which* we become intentionally identified with the essences of individual things; our knowledge of ideas, as logical entities, is indirect or reflexive, by a second intention of the mind.[37]

That Santayana exercises, without admitting, abstraction is obvious enough. The senses alone could never tell him that red is a color or B-flat a sound. Nor is it possible to intuit beauty or roundness without first abstracting such essences from existing objects that are beautiful or round. Beauty has no real existence apart from beautiful things. The mind notes many things sharing the common essence of beauty and makes a logical universal which it can then predicate of things outside the mind. Ontologically, any universal is founded in the things which participate it. But universals do not exist as such in nature or in a Platonic heaven of subsistent ideas; yet they must be determined to be such as they are by participating ideas known and determined by a creative mind.

When Santayana calls a sensible a universal he merely lifts it out of its temporal and spatial existence in nature, not however, from its singular individuation as perceived by the senses. Thus it remains singular. As long as an "essence" is *this* color or *this* sound, as he tells us, then it cannot be repeated; else it would not be *this* but something other. Hence Santayana must contradict himself as to whether essences can be repeated or not.[38]

In intellectual knowledge, Santayana stops short at simple apprehension, which is only imperfect knowledge; [39] for truth cannot be enunciated until existence is exercised in judgment. Truth or error arise only when the mind adds something of its own in making a judgment on the existence of something not itself.[40] This holds also in the case of simple sense experience. The external senses, immediately intuitive, cannot be said to be true or false, because no judgment is involved. With regard to their specific objects they cannot be deceived, unless through accidental interference; but when interpretation is made through the internal senses then a kind of sense judgment is made which is subject to truth or error.

SANTAYANA'S IDEALISM AND PRAGMATISM

From his cardinal presumption of the purely transcendental nature of knowledge, Santayana is forced into the very idealism from which he sought to escape. For he begins with wholly subjective intuition.[41] Contrary to the evidence supplied by experience, including his own, he habitually distorts the nature of man by supposing him to be a spirit imprisoned in matter.[42]

The very philosophers he criticized, especially the idealists, he followed; and he practiced precisely what he preached against:

> *Hume:* . . . his haltings and incoherence arose in the attempt to conceive experience divorced from its physical ground and from its natural objects, as a dream going on *in vacuo*. (S-AF 294.)

> *Descartes:* . . . [his] doubt was only a more penetrating use of intelligence, a sense that the alleged facts might be explained away. (S-AF 289.)

> *Kant:* An idea might by chance be the image of reality, but we could never know that it was. For the proof would have to be supplied by a further idea, and would terminate in that, the hypothesis and the corroboration would alike be mental, since experience was of ideas and could envisage nothing but the vicissitudes of the mind. (*Egotism in German Philosophy*, 35.)

> *Hegel:* The philosophy of Hegel is accordingly subjective and all its realism is but a pose and a tone wilfully assumed . . . [he] substituted so-called knowledge for being . . . not willing to confess . . . that he *was* an egotist; that it was the subjective that interested him. . . . (*Ibid.*, 86.)

Egotism: . . . arises from an exorbitant interest in ourselves, in the medium of thought and action rather than in its objects . . . the insistence on it is a little abnormal . . . a pretty sure symptom of excessive pedantry and inordinate self-assertion. (*Ibid.*, 162-163.)

Idealism . . . a mass of ill-attested and boldly dogmatic assumptions . . . Is not their criticism at bottom a work of edification or of malice, not of philosophic sincerity, so that they reject the claim to knowledge only in respect to certain physical, metaphysical or religious objects which the modern mind has become suspicious of, and hopes to feel freer without? (S-AF 295-296.)

. . . I cannot by any possibility make experience or mental discourse at large the object of investigation . . . not one term, not one conclusion in it has the least scientific value, and it is only when this philosophy is good literature that it is good for anything. (*Ibid.*, 254.)

Of William James' work on *Pragmatism*, Santayana said: "I could not stomach that way of speaking about truth." [43] But he himself was forced to conclude: "The relevance and truth of science, like the relevance and truth of sense, are pragmatic, in that they mark the actual relations, march, and distribution of events, in the terms in which they enter our experience." [44]

Santayana was too enmeshed in the philosophical errors in which he was reared, especially the heritage of radical dualism, to ever become the full-fledged realist he aspired to be. [45]

Critical Neo-Realism never succeeded in bridging the gap made by the assumption of Cartesian dualism; non-existent essences cannot build a bridge, nor does the picturesque name of "animal faith" avoid an utterly nihilistic irrationalism. [46]

"The doctrine of essences," as one critic has pointed out, ". . . works havoc in the end, because it leaves no room for existence of any kind. . . . Critical Realism lays aside all its sophistication and shows a striking capacity for a simple faith." [47] Even more to the point, the Critical Neo-Realists were doomed to failure from the beginning precisely because of their failure to be sufficiently critical of themselves. As one critic pointed out:

> They have approached the problem of knowledge burdened with a weight of prejudice that rendered antecedently impossible a satisfactory solution. The so-called "principle of immanence," at least in its pre-Kantian form, belief in materialistic evolution, negation of a transcendent, personal Deity; these and many other prejudices were accepted, in whole or in part, by the Critical Realists prior to their epistemological inquiry; certainly in the writings of none of them have these been shown to grow out of such an inquiry.[48]

SPIRITUAL FUNCTION OF ESSENCE

The aesthetic function which Santayana gives to essence is esoteric, pertinent only to a man of his solitary temperament who renounced the world as "ashes in the mouth" and the real as "rotten." If it is true that: "Every part of experience, as it comes, is illusion; and the source of this illusion is my animal nature, blindly laboring in a blind world," [49] then as he says, what is better than to "blow out the candle, and to bed"? [50]

To abstract forms from their substances, essences from existences, appearances from things, and live only in a land of illusions, arbitrarily deciding what existent facts shall be admitted and what not, is to exist as if not existing: "a blessed deliverance" for Santayana, but for all men a dangerous game of make-believe that undermines the meaning of life and glosses over the whole of reality. There is no "normal madness."

Yet in this respect of preferring the imagined to the real, Santayana said; "I think sometimes I am the only philosopher living." [51] But a philosopher is a lover of wisdom; and wisdom is grounded in real existence.

Epilogue

In Retrospect

ON MY last visit to Santayana I brought a copy of the
first draft of this manuscript. I also gave him two
books, farewell gifts, token expressions of gratitude for his
constant kindness to me during the preceding two years.

I was anxious for him to read, and react to, my critical
study of his philosophy. The books, of course, I had chosen
discriminatingly for what I considered his need and possible
benefit. One was Gilson's *Being and Some Philosophers*, because of its profound penetration of the concepts of essence
and existence. The other was Ricciotti's *Life of Christ*, selected for its excellent critical section on rationalism and
revelation. It seemed to me that these two books contained
the clearest solutions to Santayana's basic speculative problems, one philosophical and the other theological.

The mind of a man, however, cannot be abstracted from his
total personality as pure thought or speculation, an unsup-
ported and unrelated stream of consciousness. The man, in
his complete history and including all affective dispositions,
is more important, more worthy of consideration, than the
immediate state of the powers through which he thinks and
acts. Personality is dynamic as well as static, and psychoso-
matic in its expression. Mind acts through and with the body.

Santayana's problems were personal, and practical as well
as speculative. His health, or lack of it, was a pertinent fac-
tor at this time. His physical decline and disintegration af-

fected the whole organism, including a gradual loss of sight. He never read the two books I left with him, nor any more than the introductory part of this manuscript. Anyway, I doubt that even under more favorable conditions these intellectual appeals would have made much of an impression on him. It was too late.

The atmosphere of his hospital room that day accentuated the note of lateness. It was mid-afternoon, but the shades were drawn, admitting only slivers of sunlight through the blinds and across the cluttered floor. He had always been tidy, a fastidious man. Now his books and papers lay on the floor beside the deep chair in which he was slumped. The lights in his dark eyes, that customarily flickered delight or flashed concern or concentration, were dim, almost imperceptible. He stared in an empty, flat expression, reminding me of another day when I had returned some of his books and he had suddenly asked, in a dull, rhetorical tone that required no reply, "There's nothing in them worthwhile, is there?"

Now he was sick, suffering a painfully corrupting disease. He felt his own disintegration and he had begun to worry about its effects, already discernible and recognized. "I am afraid," he said, "afraid I will be bored." His usual distractions of reading and writing were becoming difficult, painful, almost impossible to him. The long conversations he had enjoyed were over. This was my last visit. And Cory, his secretary, was returning to England the following week.

He insisted on getting up and walking to the door with me. Then we stood in the doorway, silently, without fresh expression for old sentiments. His hand in mine was hard and dry and bunched, distorted by arthritic swellings. "I will not see you again," he said softly. "Now I am alone."

He had always been alone, all his life, but never so much as when he awaited death. The intestinal cancer crept through his weakened body. He could not even continue his afternoon ritual of tea and imported English cookies. In early September he tried to make one of his infrequent trips into the city of Rome. A heart attack felled him on the sidewalk and they carried him back to his room at the end of the corridor. He never left his room, or his bed, again.

There was a short interlude of apparent recovery. Sister Agatha, his faithful nurse, made her single appeal in twelve years of loving care and secret prayer. She told him that his time was running out, that he should receive a priest and make his peace with God. He mustered surprising strength to make an emphatic reply: "I have made my choice. I will die as I have lived." He forbade her to mention religion again. The injunction was unnecessary, for this was the last opportunity.

In his youth he had recognized the inevitable choice, faced by many of his contemporaries, saying: "I saw the same alternative between Catholicism and complete disillusion; but I was never afraid of disillusion, and I have chosen it." [1] The same decision was expressed poetically during his early years at Harvard:

> *And though his arms, outstretched upon the tree*
> *Were beautiful, and pleaded my embrace,*
> *My sins were loth to look upon his face.*
> *So came I down from Golgotha to Thee,*
> *Eternal Mother; let the sun and sea*
> *Heal me, and keep me in thy dwelling-place.* [2]

His choice was made early and kept to the end, at least to the end of vocal expression. His last word, spoken through the haze of a coma, was "desperation."

These indications of loneliness and religious conflict during his last days reiterated the constant themes of his whole life. The mind of Santayana cannot be analyzed apart from his personal dispositions. His philosophy was the product of his own solitude and aspirations. Solitude occasioned the development of a naturally vivid imagination, and his undeniable aspirations demanded a substitute for the moral values of a lost faith. The public result of these private concerns was a fanciful expression of philosophy, achieving sublime lyric quality, that concluded in an ultimate religion of naturalism, in the specific direction of logical essentialism.

To understand the mind of Santayana, one must know the personal history of Santayana. He was a sensitive person, profoundly impressed by physical conditions and moral tensions, a solitary and alien temperament, a stranger in all the places and circumstances of his life, a deep man who strove to fill an infinite void within himself, a man who successfully posed for others, at times even for himself, but often was disturbed by the inevitable encounter with his own ego. When he philosophized, he did not intend objective answers to common questions; he sought subjective solutions to personal problems. He permitted the publication of thirty volumes of his own composition, but only for the gain of financial security and the pleasure of recognition and reputation. His books are public records of private reflections. Whenever he wrote he was thinking out loud.

My last contact with Santayana was a letter which he wrote to me a few weeks before he died. The wavering message was scrawled on thin strips of white paper which were pasted, like the words on a telegram, onto a large lined sheet of notebook paper. The first words—"I am getting weaker and my eyes have failed me"—explained the curious composition. Only by guiding a pen along such paper-strips could a weakened and blinded writer keep his words on an even line. I will always appreciate the painstaking labor that he put into that last letter.

In retrospect, as I had written to him earlier, I had concluded that the precise keynote of his philosophy had been struck in his *Interpretations of Religion and Poetry* (1900), in which he stated that "religion was poetry intervening in life," and that all his other philosophical works were systematic elaborations of that theme. In this last letter, commenting on my retrospective observation, he admitted, "It is true that, as to religion, this book had struck the keynote."

The choice of disillusion, the rejection of the supernatural in favor of an inexplicable naturalism, could not satisfy him. He had to try to explain the inexplicable, at least to his own satisfaction. This was the task that the disillusioned poet set for himself as a philosopher. His mature system of philosophy was an attempt to integrate naturalism and justify it by reason and experience. But even more, he wanted to establish moral, even mystical, values on this foundation.

It is not surprising that he concluded with an ultimate religion of detachment from existence. He had suffered from the vicissitudes of his personal existence—"ashes in the mouth" was his own bitter description. His philosophy, therefore, was merely a matter of personal accommodation, a contrived substitution—for supernatural religion and existence, a natural religion of essentialism. Instead of adjusting to reality, he made his own world, the world of George Santayana, in which only he could live because it was situated in the depths of his own personality.

Did he succeed? Was his naturalism explained to his own satisfaction? Not with any degree of certitude, but only as a comforting persuasion. After a volume on sceptical method, he had to admit that a "solipsism of the present moment" is merely an "artificial and violent pose" and that scepticism itself is only "revised dogmatism." His own dogmas, which he had to admit were "presuppositions," were inexplicable and, taken together, irreconcilable: materialism, as to the origin of things, and subjectivism, as to the origin of ideas. The obvious difficulties that followed had to be registered as "brute facts." On his own principles, he even had to admit that his whole system of philosophy had no veridical value, only logical consistency—and this latter claim is contestable.

In the last book that he wrote, he admitted that, in his mental life, there had always been "the temptation of the primitive poet to believe his fables." He went on to speak of his enjoyment of religious inspiration, but, he said, "the temptation to mistake it for revelation was in my case never invincible." [3] These temptations were manifested often in actions that contradicted his words. For example, he liked and admired the chaplain of the hospital, although they were in opposite camps when their conversation entered the field of religion. Shortly after the chaplain's death, Santayana arranged to have a number of Masses offered for the soul of his friend!

Santayana had hoped to appeal his case to the court of common sense. His philosophy was to be founded on the common experience of men. But his subjectivism, fatal to philosophy, soon put him in the embarrassing position of a man turned inside-out. For Santayana, everything was reversed: we know thoughts before things, essences before, and separated from, existences; matter is at once potential and actual in the instant of generation; organs must find their functions; spirit comes from matter; man is an automaton, reflecting upon his own automatonism, a schizophrenic monster, an imprisoned spirit, blind to the ambient world and dreaming fanciful images with a pragmatic faith that what appears in consciousness is somehow related to reality or to extra-mental objects; the contemplative life is an escape into an ethereal region peopled by ghosts and shadows; and ultimate religion means devotion to unexisting logical being and to the dust from which we have sprung.

Is this the common sense experience of all men, the promised foundation of a philosophy, "that certain shrewd orthodoxy which the sentiment and practice of laymen maintain everywhere?" At the end of 16 years of labor in constructing his realms of being, Santayana had to admit: "In regard to my intended allegiance to common sense, I confess that in several important matters, I have not been able to maintain it." (RB-S, p. 832.)

The valid philosophical development of what is evident to common sense experience, our immediate contact with reality which logically leads to its Author, Santayana called superstition. And he dared to say: "All that is requisite in order to transform such superstition into a critical philosophy is to trace back all power to the continuous transformation of physical forces, in other words, to matter; and at the same time, by the same insight, to recognize all appearances to be mere appearances." (*Ibid.*, p. 834.) In other words, grant him his two "presuppositions" or "insights" of materialism and transcendentalism, and the rest follows. But both of these arbitrary dogmas contradict common sense experience (as well as each other), and a valid unprejudiced criticism of that experience.

In his final volume of memoirs, Santayana advised his readers: "Cultivate imagination, love it, give it endless forms, but do not let it deceive you." This is precisely what happened to a man of rare talents, perhaps even a generous touch of genius, who was deceived by the ornate imagery of his fancy into a virtual denial of all reality. Here, then, is the tragedy of genius perverted by the fatal quirks of philosophical errors. As Thomas Reid, the Scot philosopher, once remarked; "It is genius and not the want of it that adulterates philosophy."

Again, in his final work, Santayana bewailed the chaotic disintegration of his times: "The contemporary world has turned its back on the attempt and even on the desire to live reasonably. . . . Society lacks altogether that essential trait of rational living: to have a clear sanctioned ultimate aim. . . .

For the virulent cause of this long fever is subjectivism, egotism, conceit of mind." [4] These are his words; they require no comment.

Santayana's cardinal error was to posit essence as the supreme reality, perhaps the most disastrous of all metaphysical mistakes since it deprives the mind of the existent reality that is its natural and proper object. From pure essences, comprehending the quiddity of each and every being, possible or actual, real or ideal, there is no exit to existence, nor even any possible explanation for any single quiddity being what it is. "The awareness of existence," M. Gilson notes, "is the beginning of philosophical wisdom." In a technical sense, then, George Santayana never even began to be a philosopher.

His claim to recognition, to a deserved reputation, is not as a philosopher but as a poet. His philosophy belonged to him and should die with him. His exquisite literary style belongs to posterity and should live in the records of English literature. The more credit to him because English was not his native language.

Hardly anything was native to him. He was a child of mixed origins, customs, beliefs and practices. With maturity, he acquired the speculative confusion of his contemporaries. The critic may challenge the mind of Santayana in its products and publications. But the man and his responsibilities cannot be subjected to human judgment. The notion of responsibility was considered by Santayana in his commentary on Christ's condemnation of the fig tree:

> In ignoring divine prerogatives we are like the barren fig tree. Is it our fault that this is not a season for faith? Are we not doing our best, putting forth an abundance of green leaves? Do we pretend to more? Do we intentionally entice anybody to come and look for ripe fruit on our branches? Do we not wish everybody well? How then can we be cursed for not embracing unnecessary opinions that contradict all our habits of thought and judgment? Certainly we are not *to*

blame, and nature will not condemn us for any such priggish reason. It will be, if it so happens, because our further existence would not be for the glory of God. We are as innocent as the fig tree. Nevertheless it is quite possible that on the morrow we may be found withered.[5]

Notes

PART I

Introductory Note

1. *Pragmatism*, Longmans, Green & Co., 1907, p. 7.
2. *Guide to Philosophy*, Gollancz Ltd., London, 1948, p. 593.
3. Aimé Forest, cited by Donald Gallagher, in *A History of Philosophical Systems*, Vergilius Ferm, Ed., The Philosophical Library, New York, 1950, p. 456.
4. *A Discourse on Method*, Veitch, Tr., E. P. Dutton & Co., New York, 1912, p. 16.
5. *Makers of the Modern Mind*, Bruce, Milwaukee, 1949, p. 84.
6. *The Living Thought of Descartes*, Cassell & Co., Ltd., London, 1948, p. 17.
7. "My chief aim in this work has been thoroughness; and I make bold to say, that there is not a single metaphysical problem that does not find its solution, or at least the key to its solution, here." *Critique of Pure Reason*, Meiklejohn, Tr., E. P. Dutton & Co., New York, 1934, p. 3.
8. *Op. cit.*, pp. 7-8.
9. *Winds of Doctrine*, Charles Scribner's Sons, New York, 1913, p. 41.

Chapter One

1. "A General Confession," in *The Philosophy of Santayana*, vol. II, Paul A. Schilpp, Ed., The Library of Living Philosophers, p. 3. The first part of this article originally appeared in *Contemporary American Philosophers*, Adams and Montague, Eds., 1930, II, 237-57; later it appeared in *I Believe*, C. Fadiman, Ed., 1939, pp. 231-52.
2. *Persons and Places*, Constable & Co., London, 1944, p. 10.
3. *Ibid.*, p. 40.
4. *Ibid.*, p. 13.
5. *My Host the World*, Charles Scribner's Sons, New York, 1953, p. 135.
6. *Persons and Places*, p. 171.
7. *Dominations and Powers*, Charles Scribner's Sons, New York, 1951, p. 450.
8. *Persons and Places*, p. 146.
9. *Ibid.*, p. 154.

10. Brownell Baker, "The Man and the Philosopher," in *The Philosophy of Santayana*, p. 53.
11. *Persons and Places*, p. 164.
12. *Ibid.*, p. 173.
13. *Ibid.*, pp. 180-81.
14. "A General Confession," in *The Philosophy of Santayana*, p. 24.
15. *Persons and Places*, p. 92.
16. "A General Confession," in *The Philosophy of Santayana*, pp. 7-8.
17. *Persons and Places*, p. 252.
18. *The Middle Span*, Constable & Co., Ltd., London, 1947, p. 16.
19. *The Last Puritan*, Constable & Co., Ltd., London, 1935, p. 490.
20. *Persons and Places*, p. 165.
21. *The Middle Span*, p. 164.
22. *Ibid.*, p. 162.
23. Cf. Van Meter Ames, *Proust and Santayana: The Aesthetic Way of Life*, Willett Clark & Co., New York, 1937, p. 49; and Olivia H. Dunbar, "Some Critics of the English Mind," *The Yale Review*, 13:176, October, 1923.
24. *The Middle Span*, p. 167.
25. *Ibid.*, p. 170.
26. *Ibid.*, p. 165.
27. *My Host the World*, p. 2.
28. *The Middle Span*, pp. 190-91.
29. "A General Confession," in *The Philosophy of Santayana*, p. 23.
30. *Soliloquies in England*, Constable & Co., Ltd., London, 1922, p. i.
31. *Ibid.*, p. 90.
32. *Ibid.*, p. 120.
33. *Ibid.*, p. 122.
34. *Ibid.*, p. 2.
35. *Ibid.*, p. 53.
36. Daniel Cory, "Some Notes on the Deliberate Philosophy of Santayana," *Journal of Philosophy*, 47:5, March 2, 1950, p. 113.
37. *My Host the World*, p. 7.
38. Cf. *New York Times* for Dec. 17, 1951.

Chapter Two

1. In *The Philosophy of Santayana*, pp. 65-91.
2. *Persons and Places*, p. 255.
3. "A General Confession," in *The Philosophy of Santayana*, p. 15.
4. *Loc. cit.*
5. *Persons and Places*, pp. 251-52.

6. *Ibid.*, pp. 249-50.
7. *Ibid.*, pp. 246-47.
8. "A General Confession," in *The Philosophy of Santayana*, p. 9.
9. *Persons and Places*, p. 251.
10. *Ibid.*, p. 252.
11. *Ibid.*, p. 23.
12. *Egotism in German Philosophy*, Charles Scribner's Sons, New York.
13. *Soliloquies in England*, p. 216.
14. "A General Confession," in *The Philosophy of Santayana*, p. 17.
15. *Persons and Places*, p. 256.
16. *Scepticism and Animal Faith*, Constable & Co., Ltd., London, 1923, pp. 298-300.
17. *The Middle Span*, p. 160.
18. *Ibid.*, pp. 160-61.
19. *Soliloquies in England*, p. 216.
20. *The Middle Span*, p. 162.
21. *Scepticism and Animal Faith*, p. 290.
22. *The Middle Span*, pp. 165-66.
23. *Ibid.*, p. 13.
24. *Scepticism and Animal Faith*, p. 306.
25. *Soliloquies in England*, pp. 214-15.
26. *Scepticism and Animal Faith*, p. viii.
27. "A General Confession," in *The Philosophy of Santayana*, p. 8.
28. "Apologia Pro Mente Sua," in *The Philosophy of Santayana*, p. 604.

Chapter Three

1. Cf. William P. Montague, "The Story of American Realism," in *Twentieth Century Philosophy*, D. Runes, Ed., Philosophical Library, New York, 1947, pp. 419-48.
2. *Ibid.*, p. 423.
3. *Ibid.*, p. 436.
4. *Ibid.*, p. 419.
5. Roy Wood Sellars, "What is the Correct Interpretation of Critical Realism?", *Journal of Philosophy*, 24:9, April 28, 1927, p. 238.
6. *Op. cit.*, p. 441.
7. *Ibid.*, p. 443.
8. B. H. Bode, "Critical Realism," *Journal of Philosophy*, 19:3, Feb. 2, 1922, p. 70.
9. *Essays in Critical Realism*, Macmillan Co., New York, 1920, note, p. 4.
10. *Loc. cit.*

PART II

Introductory Note

1. *Scepticism and Animal Faith*, p. vi.
2. *The Middle Span*, p. 16.
3. *Ibid.*, p. 156.
4. *Reason in Common Sense*, Charles Scribner's Sons, New York, 1905, p. 6.
5. *Soliloquies in England*, p. 251.
6. *Poems*, Constable & Co., Ltd., London, 1922, pp. xii-xiii.
7. *The Last Puritan*, p. 687.
8. *The Middle Span*, p. 164.
9. *Scepticism and Animal Faith*, p. v.
10. *Ibid.*, p. vii.
11. *Ibid.*, p. vi.
12. To simplify reference to these five books, so frequently cited, abbreviations will be used. S-AF signifies *Scepticism and Animal Faith*, in the edition already noted. On Santayana's recommendation, I used the single-volume edition of *Realms of Being*, published by Charles Scribner's Sons, New York, 1942, which contains a new introduction and a postscript by Santayana. RB, then, signifies *Realms of Being*, in this edition, and I will add in parentheses the initial letter of the single books that comprise the volume: (E) *The Realm of Essence;* (M) *The Realm of Matter;* (S) *The Realm of Spirit;* (T) *The Realm of Truth.*

Chapter One

1. RB, Intro., p. xxv.
2. RB (E), pp. 3-4.
3. *Ibid.*, p. 4.
4. *Ibid.*, p. 15.
5. S-AF, p. vi.
6. *Ibid.*, pp. xxvii-xxviii.

Chapter Two

1. Cf. "Literal and Symbolic Knowledge," in *The Journal of Philosophy, Psychology, and Scientific Methods*, 15, Aug. 1, 1912, pp. 421-44. Reference to essence was made in some of his essays which later were published in *Soliloquies in England*. Many of these had appeared previously in English and American journals.

2. S-AF, p. 77.
3. RB (E), p. 22.
4. *Ibid.*, p. 2.
5. S-AF, p. 39.
6. RB (E), p. 5.
7. *Ibid.*, p. 18; cf. also S-AF, p. 93 and p. 116.
8. RB (E), p. 19.
9. *Essays in Critical Realism*, note, p. 168.
10. Alfred N. Whitehead, whose concept of an "eternal object" is similar to Santayana's notion of essence, speaks in the same manner: "Thus every so-called 'universal' is particular in the sense of being just what it is, diverse from everything else; and every so-called 'particular' is universal in the sense of entering into the constitution of other actual entities." *Process and Reality*, Cambridge ed., New York, 1929, p. 66.
11. RB (E), p. 22.
12. *Ibid.*, p. 78.
13. S-AF, p. 112.
14. RB (E), p. 26.
15. *Ibid.*, p. 27.
16. "It is as the forms things wear to the senses or to the practical intellect that essences are first noticed." *Ibid.*, p. 30.
17. "This recognition that the data of experience are essences is Platonic, but it is corrective of all that is sentimental in Platonism, curing it as it were homoeopathetically. . . . Although essences have the texture and ontological status of Platonic ideas, they can lay claim to none of the cosmological, metaphysical or moral prerogatives attributed to those ideas. They are infinite in number and neutral in value." S-AF, p. 78.
18. RB (E), p. 34.
19. "But such an approach [the previous apprehension of a particular round object] is accidental: a true psychologist would often record that in looking at some roundish thing he first noticed and intuited nothing but roundness, perfect, Platonic, and unadulterated." *Ibid.*, pp. 34-35.
20. *Ibid.*, p. 36.
21. *Ibid.*, pp. 41-42.
22. *Ibid.*, p. 40.
23. S-AF, p. 241; RB (E), p. 44.
24. "So when a human eye is turned skyward, the sky truly acquires the quality of looking blue and round: those are its real qualities in relation to such an observer, as certain substances are truly poison for rats." RB (E), p. 44.
25. S-AF, p. 167.

26. RB (E), p. 45.
27. *Ibid.*, p. 47.
28. *Ibid.*, pp. 48-49.
29. *Ibid.*, p. 57.
30. *Ibid.*, p. 71.
31. *Ibid.*, p. 82.
32. *Loc. cit.*
33. RB (E), p. 90.
34. "... Although essence is everywhere present it never occurs alone, but either as the form of some existing thing or event, or else as a term given in intuition." RB (M), p. 382.
35. *Ibid.*, p. 294.
36. RB (E), p. 129.
37. *Ibid.*, pp. 148-50.
38. From a personal letter to the author, dated Feb. 26, 1952.
39. S-AF, p. 92.
40. *Ibid.*, p. 54.
41. RB (M), p. 254.
42. S-AF, p. 151.
43. RB (E), p. 37.
44. *Ibid.*, p. 9.
45. "Thus intuition of essences first enables the mind to say something about anything, to think of what is not given, and to be a mind at all." *Ibid.*, p. 82.

Chapter Three

1. "Transcendental Absolutism," in *Twentieth Century Philosophy*, p. 315.
2. S-AF, p. 49.
3. RB (M), p. 204.
4. *Ibid.*, p. 193.
5. *Ibid.*, p. 200.
6. *Ibid.*, p. 206.
7. S-AF, pp. 190-91.
8. *Ibid.*, pp. 205-06.
9. *Ibid.*, pp. 201, 209. Yet in other instances, Santayana includes not only physical things under the notion of substance, but also spiritual "entities as such," intuitions themselves, and instants of consciousness. Cf. S-AF, p. 47. Also: "every event, even if wholly psychological or phenomenal, is a substance. It is a self-subsisting fact, open to description. . . ." *Ibid.*, p. 182.
10. S-AF, p. 208.
11. RB (M), p. 234; cf. also RB (E), p. 51.

12. S-AF, p. 217.

13. RB (M), p. 189.

14. *Ibid.*, p. 183.

15. *Loc. cit.*

16. RB (M), p. 187.

17. *Ibid.*, p. 189.

18. *Ibid.*, p. 292.

19. *Loc. cit.*

20. RB (S), p. 578.

21. RB (M), p. 219.

22. RB (S), p. 555.

23. "Essences, by being eternally what they are, enable existence to pass from one phase to another, and enable the mind to note and describe the change." RB (E), p. 5.

24. "Even these instances of essence which are not forms of substance in this passive manner, are manifestations of substance by way of active expression or epigenesis; though not embodied in substance they are evoked from it and compose the realm of spirit, which is a natural manifestation of substance in man, but not a true description of it." RB (M), *loc. cit.*

25. RB (M), p. 294.

26. *Ibid.*, pp. 275-76.

27. RB (E), pp. 109-10.

28. RB (M), p. 218.

29. *Soliloquies in England*, p. 142.

30. S-AF, p. 208.

31. RB (M), p. 276.

32. *Loc. cit.*

33. RB (M), p. 291.

34. "The mysterious potentiality packed in the seed would then not be internal to it, or due to a specially wonderful essence therein embodied. It would be the concentration there of many external relations at work together, a resultant of all the cosmic tensions to which that point was subject." *Ibid.*, p. 290.

35. RB (M), p. 347.

36. *Ibid.*, p. 291.

37. A form changes "when the balance of tensions which brought it about yields to a fresh equilibrium." *Ibid.*, p. 292.

38. RB (T), p. 417.

39. RB (M), p. 301.

40. *Loc. cit.*

41. RB (E), p. 155.

42. "The tropes which we call the laws of nature cannot there-

fore exclude other and contrary manifestations of what nature secretly contains." RB (M), p. 307.

43. RB (M), p. 304.

44. *Ibid.*, p. 303.

45. RB (T), p. 412.

46. RB (M), p. 323.

47. "Nature is full of coiled springs and predestined rhythms; of mechanisms so wound up that, as soon as circumstances permit, they unroll themselves through a definite series of phases." *Loc. cit.*

48. RB (M), pp. 325-26.

49. Santayana insists he is not a materialist in the sense that the only reality is matter, but that whatever exists has its origin in matter. Cf. "Apologia Pro Mente Sua," in *The Philosophy of Santayana,* p. 509.

50. "By the word matter I do not understand any human idea of matter, popular or scientific, ancient or recent." *Ibid.*, p. 332.

51. *Loc. cit.*

52. ". . . it is the object of biology." RB (M), p. 333.

53. Cf. RB (E), p. 97; RB (M), pp. 328-54; S-AF, pp. 152, 250; *Soliloquies in England,* pp. 218-24. In this last place, Santayana imaginatively pictures the psyche blindly existing in the depths of the body, and begetting, in a process of evolution, conscious intuition.

54. S-AF, pp. 274-75. Yet, elsewhere he speaks of spirit's reflexive ability to observe itself: "it can even view itself" etc. Cf. RB (S), p. 556.

55. RB (M), p. 331.

56. *Ibid.*, p. 348.

57. "The psyche remains a mystery in her intrinsic operations; and if something of that mystery seems to hang about the feminine name we are giving her, so much the better: we are warned that we do not, and probably cannot, understand." *Ibid.*, p. 335.

58. S-AF, p. 109.

59. RB (M), p. 194.

60. RB (T), p. 441.

61. RB (E), p. 161.

Chapter Four

1. Cf. S-AF, p. 170.

2. "Nothing given is either physical or mental, in the sense of being intrinsically a thing or a thought; it is just a quality of being." *Ibid.*, p. 92.

3. *Ibid.*, p. 193. Elsewhere, however, Santayana attributes some cognitive value to intuition: "It belongs to the nature of spirit to be

cognitive; for even when intuition is pure and unmixed with intent, so that there is no claim to transitive knowledge, no positing of facts, intuition must reveal an object other than its own spiritual being and activity." RB (E), p. 129.

4. "Sensation and thought (between which there is no essential difference) work in a conventional medium, as do literature and music." S-AF, p. 102.

5. *Ibid.*, pp. 91-92.

6. Cf. S-AF, pp. 92-93.

7. "The intrinsic action of spirit . . . cannot be itself an object of intuition. . . ." RB (E), p. 129.

8. "Knowledge is one species of faith." S-AF, p. 167. Santayana devotes a whole chapter of this work (VIII) to this thesis.

9. RB, Intro., p. xxviii.

10. ". . . animal faith, when it describes in suitable symbols . . . the objects encountered in action, is what I call knowledge." RB (E), p. 4.

11. S-AF, p. 81.

12. "The occasions on which spirit arises in man are the vicissitudes of his animal life. . . ." *Ibid.*, p. 276. Also, in speaking of intuition of essences: "These spiritual perspectives are called forth only occasionally, as matter rolls on. . . ." RB (E), p. 134.

13. S-AF, p. 86.

14. *Ibid.*, p. 88.

15. RB (E), p. 130. Santayana notes here that he uses the term *objective* in the original scholastic sense.

16. S-AF, p. 276.

17. "How should the essences, mainly emotional and inwardly elicited, which events evoke in this or that sensitive organism, reveal substance in its inmost constitution and total extent?" RB (E), p. 161.

18. RB (E), p. 131.

19. *Ibid.*, p. 134.

20. *Ibid.*, p. 135; cf. also p. 125.

21. *Loc. cit.*

22. S-AF, pp. 84-85.

23. "The notion of essence also relieves the weary philosopher of several other problems, even more scholastic and artificial, concerning sensations and ideas, particulars and universals, the abstract and the concrete. There are no such differences in essences as they are given." *Ibid.*, p. 90.

24. S-AF, pp. 82-83. Also: "All this confusion comes of originally supposing that things are graphically copied in sense, and nature in science; a belief founded on the projection of the essences given to

spirit, as if the world had been created and were now deployed on the model of human ideas." RB (E), p. 136.
25. RB (E), pp. 108-09.
26. *Ibid.*, p. 112.
27. *Ibid.*, p. 115.
28. *Ibid.*, p. 35.
29. S-AF, p. 208.
30. RB (E), p. 110. A pictorial expression of the same proposition: "The whole rumble of the discoursing mind is music on the march, and no sane man expects it to join in battle or to describe an enemy." *Ibid.*, p. 113.
31. RB (E), p. 99.
32. *Ibid.*, p. 98.
33. *Loc. cit.*
34. S-AF, p. 119. Elsewhere logic is referred to as "a kind of rhetoric. It marshals intuitions in ways which are irrelevant to them." RB (E), p. 90.
35. S-AF, p. 118.
36. RB (E), p. 125.
37. *Ibid.*, p. 158. Also cf. S-AF, p. 167.
38. RB (M), p. 350.
39. S-AF, p. 167. With characteristic picturesque prose, Santayana describes the sounded word as "the claw with which intent clutches the potent fact." RB (E), p. 112.
40. S-AF, p. 167.
41. *Loc. cit.*
42. *Ibid.*
43. *Ibid.*
44. "So long as a knowledge is demanded that shall be intuition the issue can only be laughter or despair; for if I attain intuition, I have only a phantom object, and if I spurn that and turn to the facts, I have renounced intuition." S-AF, p. 170.
45. S-AF, pp. 169-70.
46. *Loc. cit.*
47. The notion of bodily attitude localizing intention is proposed also by Roy Wood Sellars, a collaborator with Santayana in *Essays in Critical Realism*.
48. ". . . the aesthetic and sentimental essences which fill human discourse . . . *cannot* be true, save in the historical sense that it may be true that someone has entertained them." RB (E), p. 131.
49. RB (T), p. 420.
50. *Character and Opinion in the United States*, Constable & Co., Ltd., London, 1920, pp. 153-55.
51. *Ibid.*, p. 155.

Chapter Five

1. "Apologia Pro Mente Sua," in *The Philosophy of Santayana*, p. 500.

2. *Platonism and the Spiritual Life*, Charles Scribner's Sons, New York, 1927, p. 38.

3. ". . . images have other properties and other uses for the spirit beside their value as signals relevant to action. They have intrinsic form; and precisely because they are in a manner illusions, they are originals; ideal objects interesting in themselves. In themselves they are essences without existence." *Dominations and Powers*, p. 21.

4. *Soliloquies in England*, p. 197.

5. "I think that pure reason in the naturalist may attain, without subterfuge, all the spiritual insights which supernaturalism goes so far out of the way to inspire." *The Genteel Tradition at Bay*, Charles Scribner's Sons, New York, 1931, p. 64.

6. *Ibid.*, pp. 73-74.

7. RB (S), p. 646.

8. *Ibid.*, p. 643.

9. "The flux of things is terrible indeed to the distracted spirit, compelled to cling and tremble and whine at the mutations of matter; but those mutations themselves become musical and comic, if once the spirit can free itself and perceive its affinity to the eternal." *Ibid.*, p. 687.

10. Like a Greek sage, Santayana says: "Health and knowledge; essentially nothing more is requisite for liberation from distraction by the flesh, the world, and the devil." RB (S), p. 749. Negatively, the sleeping child illustrates this placid liberation, enjoying as he does life without distraction and untaxed natural health. Eventually the liberation of spirit is achieved by a mature and awake childlike innocence. "Spirituality is only a sort of return to innocence, birdlike and childlike." *The Genteel Tradition at Bay*, p. 64.

11. Unlike Santayana, St. John of the Cross "had not intellectual or historical lights to show him the whole system of Christianity from the outside, as one figment of imagination among many." RB (S), p. 755.

12. *Loc. cit.*

13. *Ibid.*, p. 774.

14. *Ibid.*, p. 810.

15. RB (E), p. 12.

16. RB (S), p. 825.

17. *Ibid.*, p. 845.

18. RB (S), p. 846.

19. *Loc. cit.*

20. RB (S), p. 847.
21. *Ibid.*, p. 827.
22. Contained under "Obiter Scripta," in *The Philosophy of Santayana*, Irwin Edman, Ed., Modern Library, Random House, New York, 1942, pp. 581-93.
23. Charles Scribner's Sons, New York, 1946.
24. This is the last book Santayana wrote. The third volume of his memoirs, *My Host the World*, although published posthumously, was written many years before his death. The single volume revised edition of *The Life of Reason*, recently published, is an abridgement of the original work, initiated and directed by Santayana but worked out and completed by Mr. Daniel Cory.
25. *Interpretations of Poetry and Religion*, Charles Scribner's Sons, New York, 1900. His first book publication was *The Sense of Beauty* (Scribner's, 1896); the second to appear was *Lucifer, A Theological Tragedy* (H. S. Stone & Co., Chicago, 1899).
26. RB (E), p. 58.

PART III

Introductory Note

1. Sr. M. Cyril Edwin Kinney, O.P., *A Critique of the Philosophy of George Santayana in the Light of Thomistic Principles*, The Catholic University Press, Washington, D.C., 1942.
2. P. Norbertus Oldegeering, O.F.M., *Georgius Santayana et Problema Epistemologicum*, Antonianum, Rome, 1950. Another critical study, recently published, was done at the Sorbonne by M. Jacques Duron (*La pensée de George Santayana*, Nizet, Paris, 1950). M. Duron, however, has concentrated his study on the original edition of the *Life of Reason*, of which Santayana said, "There is hardly a page that would not need to be rewritten to express my present opinion. . . ." Cf. *Living Authors*, D. Tante, Ed., H. W. Wilson Co., New York, 1931, p. 359. As noted, an abridgement and revision, edited by Daniel Cory, appeared after the death of Santayana.
3. ". . . I should dislike to frame an unprecedented opinion, unless at least I thought it more congruous with common sense." RB (S), p. 828. "This system would be a revision of the categories of common sense . . . endeavoring only to clarify those categories. . . ." *Ibid.*, p. 826. "I have a great respect for orthodoxy . . . a certain shrewd orthodoxy which the sentiment and practice of laymen maintain everywhere. I think that common sense, in a rough dogged way, is sounder than the special schools of philosophy. . . ." S-AF, p. v. "Fortunately exact science and the books of the learned are not nec-

essary to establish my essential doctrine: for it rests on public experience." *Ibid.*, p. x.

4. "Apologia Pro Mente Sua," in *The Philosophy of Santayana*, p. 499.

5. RB (S), p. 827.

6. "Apologia Pro Mente Sua," in *The Philosophy of Santayana*, p. 604. Also "unfortunately . . . my own fancy is too spontaneous, interfering with an accurate and orderly exposition of facts and arguments. . . . I like theories and arguments when they are spontaneous and not used to refute one another; but they come to me as refinements or excursions." RB (S), pp. 826-27. Along with this difficulty of ornate expression, is Santayana's frequent use, or, rather, misuse, of Scholastic terminology, which often misleads an unsuspecting reader.

7. See the passage from his "Apologia," used on the introductory page to this section. From "Apologia Pro Mente Sua," in *The Philosophy of Santayana*, p. 605.

8. S-AF, p. 15.

9. RB (T), p. 418.

10. S-AF, p. x.

11. RB (T), p. 419.

12. RB (S), p. 826. This summary passage merits complete citation: "Nor does it escape being, in effect, a system of the universe, since the realm of matter, conceived mechanically, here forms the groundwork of all existence, the realm of spirit being only a sort of invisible vegetation flourishing in some of the stars, and the realm of truth a history of those happenings, while the realm of essence is but an infinite void presupposed, a part of which is occupied by the other realities."

13. S-AF, p. vi.

14. RB, Pref., p. xxix.

Chapter One

1. *Persons and Places*, p. 255.

2. "Living when human faith is again in a state of dissolution, I have imitated the Greek sceptics in calling doubtful everything that, in spite of common sense, any one can possibly doubt." S-AF, p. 308.

3. *Ibid.*, p. 305. Cf. also S-AF, p. viii and p. 306; RB (S), pp. 827-28.

4. Cf. S-AF, p. 306.

5. *Ibid.*, p. 1.

6. *Ibid.*, p. 2.

7. In speaking of first principles, the primary and necessary postulates of judgment, we are referring to the fundamental basis of all thought and action, the principle of contradiction, and those consequent principles immediately inferred: the principle of identity, the positive affirmation following the principle of contradiction; the principle of sufficient reason, responsible for the realm of existing essences; the principle of the excluded middle (no medium between being and non-being); the principle of inequality (the basis of the relational syllogism, such as the application of the maxim: the whole is greater than its parts.) I have noted elsewhere Santayana's failure to grasp the significance of the principle of sufficient reason, missing the proper emphasis on sufficiency: a sufficient foundation for an essence existing rather than non-existing; obviously there must be a *raison d'être*, else there would be no *être*, nor could we distinguish being from non-being, something from nothing.

8. James B. Sullivan, *First Principles in Thought and Being*, The Catholic University of America Press, Washington, D.C., 1939, p. 29. The reference to Hume follows: "The *intense* view of these manifold contradictions and imperfections in human reason has so wrought upon me, and heated my brain, that I am ready to reject all belief and reasoning, and can look upon no opinion even as more probable or likely than another. . . . I dine, I play a game of backgammon, I converse, and am merry with my friends; and when, after three or four hours' amusement, I would return to these speculations, they appear so cold, and strained, and ridiculous, that I cannot find in my heart to enter into them any further." *A Treatise of Human Nature*, Bk. I, Part IV, Sect. VII, *Philosophical Works*, Little Brown, Boston, 1854, vol. I, 331.

9. *Metaph.*, Bk. XI (K), c. 5, p. 1061b, 34 ff.

10. S-AF, p. 10.

11. *Ibid.*, p. 11.

12. *Ibid.*, p. 290.

13. Cf. S-AF, pp. 298-300.

14. *The Living Thought of Descartes*, pp. 19-20.

15. *Illi qui volunt inquirere veritatem, non considerando prius dubitationem, assimulantur illis qui nesciunt quo vadant. Et hoc ideo, quia sicut terminus viae est illud quod intenditur ab ambulante, ita exclusio dubitationis est finis qui intenditur ab inquirante veritatem. Manifestum est autem quod ille qui nescit quo vadat, non potest directe ire, nisi forte a casu: ergo nec aliquis potest directe inquirere veritatem, nisi prius videat dubitationem.* S. Thomas, in III *Metaph.*, lect. 1, Marietti, 1950, p. 97.

St. Thomas, speaking of metaphysics, says: *Ista scientia, sicut habet universalem considerationem de veritate, ita etiam ad eam per-*

tinet universalis dubitatio de veritate. Ibid. Some have seen in this phrase, out of context, an approval of universal doubt in the extreme sense of *de omnibus est dubitandum.* But the Angelic Doctor here is explaining Aristotle's teaching on the necessity of considering difficulties: *bene dubitare.* Since metaphysics considers universal truth, it must defend, by its principles, all the other sciences whenever truth is jeopardized. There is no reflection of doubt on the ability of the mind to attain certitude, rather, there is an assertion of the mind's veridical value. Cf. Paul Farrell, O.P., "Portals of Doubt," *The Thomist,* 8:3, July 1945, pp. 293-368.

16. Cf. *De Veritate,* q. 10, a. 8, Marietti, Rome, 1949, p. 205.
17. S-AF, p. 40.
18. RB (M), p. 195.
19. S-AF, pp. 8-9.
20. RB (T), p. 466.
21. *Ibid.,* p. 528.
22. RB (E), p. 18.
23. RB (E), p. 18.
24. S-AF, p. 35.
25. *Ibid.,* pp. 39-40.
26. *Ibid.,* p. 39.
27. "We must oscillate between a radical transcendentalism, frankly reduced to a solipsism of the living moment, and a materialism posited as a presupposition of conventional sanity." "A General Confession," in *The Philosophy of Santayana,* p. 17. "I agreed with his [Spencer's] naturalism or materialism, because that is what we all start with: the minimum presupposition of perception and action." *Persons and Places,* pp. 249-50.
28. In a characteristic circumlocution, he says: "Not that naturalism must be true *a priori,* but that nature sets the standard of naturalness." Cf. *Persons and Places,* pp. 246-47.
29. *Ibid.,* p. 179.
30. "A General Confession," in *The Philosophy of Santayana,* p. 17.
31. *Soliloquies in England,* p. 223.
32. S-AF, p. 110.
33. *Persons and Places, loc. cit.*
34. I have paraphrased here a passage from the excellent treatise on criticism by E. T. Toccafondi, O.P. *Il vero metodo è la via che guida il pensiero nel suo svolgersi e nel suo organizzarsi secondo le esigenze della sua natura. La riflessione segue la natura. Il metodo aiuta il pensiero nel raggiungimento del suo fine naturale: la conquista della verità. Non è quindi e non può esser buon metodo, quello che svia il pensiero dal suo fine naturale. Affermato dunque l'essere come necessario all'umano conoscere, è un errore di metodo dichi-*

ararne, prima dell'esame critico, l'immanenza assoluta o presupporre, senza alcun controllo, la trascendenza riguardo al pensiero. È *infatti proprio questa la questione da risolvere; e la soluzione deve esser frutto e risultato dell'indagine critica. La Ricerca Critica Della Realità,* Arnodo, Rome, 1941, p. 57.

35. "A General Confession," in *The Philosophy of Santayana,* pp. 17-18.

36. S-AF, p. 306.

37. *Si vous prenez votre point de départ dans la pensée, vous n'en sortirez plus, vous y resterez enfermé; ce fut le malheur de Descartes; ce sera le destin de tous ceux qui se risqueront à le suivre.*
. . . *La leçon est claire, nous dit-on; abandonnez donc cette voie dangereuse; suivez l'example des anciens, des Grecs, d'Aristote, des scolastiques, de saint Thomas. Au point de départ de la philosophie, il vous faut admettre les choses, comme ils l'ont fait. C'est un postulat nécessaire.* L. Noel, *Le realisme immediat,* Louvain, 1938, p. 103.

38. S-AF, p. 193.

39. RB, Pref., p. xxix.

40. S-AF, p. 304.

41. S-AF, p. 28.

Chapter Two

1. ". . . intuition of itself is intransitive . . . having no object other than the datum. . . ." S-AF, p. 262. "From the transcendental point of view, which is that of spirit, substance is an unobtainable goal, or object-as-such, being posited, not possessed." *Ibid.,* p. 206; cf. also RB (S), p. 816, S-AF, p. 103; *Ibid.,* p. 185.

2. *Ibid.,* p. 35. Yet he says later on: "Although a sceptic may doubt all existence, none being involved in any indubitable datum, yet I think good human reasons, apart from irresistible impulse, can be found for positing existing intuitions to which data appear, no less than other existing events and things, which the intuited data report or describe." S-AF, pp. 49-50. This appeal to "human reasons" enables Santayana to get out of the circle of solipsism at the expense of an about-face which might as well have been made from the beginning. There are good human reasons, self-evident, for our immediate contact, implicit but immediate, with existence. To deny our contact with "external relations" is first to recognize them and distinguish them from internal relations.

3. RB (S), p. 831.

4. S-AF, pp. 110-11.

5. S-AF, p. 48.

6. *Ibid.,* p. 42.

7. Cf. RB (E), Chapters V and VI; also "Some Meanings of the Word *Is*," *Journal of Philosophy*, 21:14, July 3, 1924. In this article, Santayana assigns identity to the first position of meaning, existence to fifth place.

8. RB (E), p. 5. "Whenever I use the word *is*, except in sheer tautology, I deeply misuse it. . . ." S-AF, p. 71.

9. St. Thomas treats the immediate intellectual experience of being in: *Summa Theologica*, Ia, q. 4, a. 2; Ia, q. 85, a. 3; Ia-IIae, q. 94, a. 2; *Contra Gentes*, II, 83; *De Veritate*, q. 1, a. 1; *De Anima*, II, 6, lect. 13.

10. Cf. *Comm.* in Ia, q. 82, a. 3.

11. Santayana himself observes: "If you are a materialist in respect to matter, you will be an idealist in respect to mind." "Transcendental Absolutism," in *Twentieth Century Philosophy*, pp. 319-20.

12. The same indication appears in Santayana's description of the relation of essence to pure being: "Pure Being is . . . that which all essences have in common—namely character or distinguishableness and self-identity. . . ." RB (T), p. 429.

13. "If a thing has being, or definite character, it also lacks being, because in being what it is it rejects and banishes all that it is not, so that all positive wealth is shadowed by privation." RB (T), p. 429.

14. Etienne Gilson, *Being and Some Philosophers*, The Pontifical Institute of Mediaeval Studies, Toronto, 1949, p. 19.

15. ". . . it is only a dark principle, transcendental in respect to the datum . . . that calls up this datum at all, or leads me to posit its existence." S-AF, p. 52; ". . . by the intervention of irrational power . . . the infinity of essence is determined to a particular complex or series of forms." RB (S), p. 847. (From an immaterial essence, alone self-evident, Santayana leaps to a dark principle, matter, to explain all things, including essences!)

16. "In like manner, the good may be said to be not only the author of knowledge to all things known, but of their being and essence, and yet the good is not essence, but far exceeds essence in dignity and power." *Republic*, Bk. VI, Jowett Ed., Random House, New York, vol. 1, 770.

17. Jacques Maritain, *A Preface to Metaphysics*, Sheed & Ward, New York, 1948, pp. 37-38.

18. *Op. cit.*, p. 121.

19. We might as well ask Santayana what he means by "the mind's eye" (S-AF, p. 86). Does the mind (which he identifies with spirit) have an eye?

20. RB (S), p. 837.

21. *Op. cit.*, pp. 202-03.

22. RB (E), p. 34.

23. *Soliloquies in England,* p. 256.

24. *Op. cit.,* p. 215.

25. Cf., for example, matter's causality of forms: Chapters V, VI in RB (M), pp. 267-309. In the very next chapter, causality is denied.

26. "Blind spontaneity must generate, and not make, the instruments and the goals of deliberate action." RB (S), p. 847. Organs, he tells us, arise spontaneously and for no reason except circumstantial "tensions." As for "precision of adjustment between organs and functions . . . nothing has any functions but those which it has come to have, when plasticity here with stimulus and opportunity there have conspired to establish them." RB (M), pp. 321-22. This is the substitution Santayana offers for what he called "absurd reasonings."

27. RB (S), p. 846.

28. "The ignorant . . . imagine that the four principles (which they call causes) are all equally forces producing change and co-operative sources of natural things. . . . These learned babblers would put nature together out of words, and would regard the four principles of interpretation as forces mutually supplementary, combining to produce natural things: as if perfection could be one of the sources of imperfection, or as if the form which things happen to have could be one of the causes of their having it." Avicenna speaking in *Dialogues in Limbo,* Charles Scribner's Sons, New York, 1941, pp. 238-39.

29. RB (T), p. 420.

30. *Character and Opinion in the United States,* p. 153.

31. Cf. S-AF, pp. 267-68.

32. RB (T), p. 417.

33. *Ibid.,* p. 408.

34. For further discussion of inconsistencies and circular argumentation in Santayana's philosophy of essence, cf. Mary Calkins, "On Certain Difficulties in the Modern Doctrine of Essence," *Journal of Philosophy,* 23:26, Dec. 23, 1926.

35. RB (E), p. 30; cf also *ibid.,* p. 23.

36. *Ibid.,* p. 40.

37. "Some Observations on the Philosophy of Santayana," in *The Philosophy of Santayana,* pp. 102-03.

38. That which the intellect first grasps as most known (*notissimum—De Verit.,* q. I, a. 1) is being; an essence perfected by the act of existence, an act apprehended as signified in simple apprehension and as exercized in judgment.

In finite beings, existence is not of the essence of its being (otherwise they would always exist) but really distinct from it, as act from potency. Contingent beings, since they participate existence, manifest a self-sufficient Being, whose very essence is to exist.

Being is either real, existing in the nature of things, or merely a being of reason (which is not, strictly speaking, a being but only conceived as such). Real being is either actual or possible, the latter not altogether removed from existence because possibilities are determined by divine choice and, in a sense, exist as a divine idea. (*De Verit.*, q. II, a. 5).

All real beings are either substances, properly existing in themselves, or accidents, whose natural being is to exist in something else, and, as Aristotle pointed out, are more properly said to belong to rather than to be beings. (*Summa Theol.*, Ia, q. 45, a. 4).

Every finite substance, subject to change, manifests a potential substratum (prime matter) and distinguishable determination (substantial form); as well as a secondary, perceptible matter, quantitatively individuated, and an apparent, accidental form.

Essence is restricted to what is expressed by definition of a substance, composed of both matter and form. St. Thomas says: "Strictly speaking, the essence is what is expressed by the definition. Now, the definition comprises the principles of the species, but not the individual principles. Hence, in things composed of matter and form, the essence signifies not the form alone, nor the matter alone, but what is composed of matter and the common form, as the principles of the species." (*Essentia proprie est id quod significatur per definitionem. Definitio autem complectitur principia speciei, non autem principia individualia. Unde in rebus compositis ex materia et forma, essentia significat non solum formam, nec solum materiam, sed compositum ex materia et forma communi, prout sunt principia speciei. Summa Theol.*, IIIa, q. 29, a. 2, ad 3um.)

St. Thomas also points out, however, that among the ancient philosophers essence is sometimes called *quiddity*, since a definition expresses what a thing is; sometimes *form*, in as much as form is the determining principle in a substance; and sometimes *nature*, indicating an essence as a source of operation or function. But, strictly speaking, essence should be reserved for the meaning given above. Cf. *De Ente et Essentia*, c. 1, *Opuscula Omnia*, Lethielleus, Paris, 1941, t. 1, p. 26.

39. "Because we must take our knowledge of simpler elements from composites and come to what is prior from what is posterior, so that beginning with simpler things study may be more suitable, we should proceed from the meaning of being to the meaning of essence." (*Quia vero ex compositis simplicium cognitionem accipere debemus et ex posterioribus in priora devenire, ita facilioribus incipientes conveni-*

entior fiat disciplina, ideo ex significatione entis ad significationem essentiae procedendum est. De Ente et Essentia, c. 1, ed. cit., p. 25.)

40. *Omnis errans circa principia omnium intelligibilium magis errabit circa alia; omnis errans circa essentiam et ens errat circa principia omnium intelligibilium; ergo omnis errans circa essentiam et ens magis errabit circa alia. Comm. in De Ente et Essentia,* Proemium, Marietti, Rome, 1934, p. 1.

Chapter Three

1. Santayana makes a definite distinction between essences incorporated in existents and those which appear in intuition: the former are actual, the latter are specious. The specious essence is not derived from essences realized in nature since "Nothing existent can appear, and nothing specious can exist." S-AF, p. 63. "Essences may have the ideal status of an object of intuition now, and again the material status of the form of a thing." RB (E), p. 167.

2. "Matter here means the *essence* which some philosopher attributes . . . to matter which has probably suggested itself to the philosopher after much consideration of the ways of nature . . . but no essence can be the origin of anything . . . real matter . . . is not anybody's *idea* of matter." RB (E), p. 140. To which a critic can add: least of all a transcendental philosopher unable to achieve transitive knowledge and reducing all knowledge to mere belief.

3. Will Durant, *The Story of Philosophy,* Garden City Co., New York, 1943, p. 371.

4. S-AF, p. 80.

5. RB (E), p. 6.

6. *Ibid.,* p. 20.

7. *Ibid.,* p. 9.

8. *Loc. cit.* By a sort of reverse abstraction, Santayana says that: "By spirit essences are transposed into appearances." S-AF, p. 274. Elsewhere we are told that essences *are* appearances, or that appearances have to be stripped to expose an essence.

9. S-AF, p. 86.

10. RB (E), p. 30.

11. RB (M), p. 351.

12. S-AF, p. 167.

13. Marten Ten Hoor, "Santayana's Theory of Knowledge," in *Journal of Philosophy,* 20:8, April 12, 1923, p. 201.

14. *Essays in Critical Realism,* p. 183. Cf. also S-AF, p. 165.

15. S-AF, p. 88.

16. *Ibid.,* p. 9.

17. RB (S), p. 847.

18. RB (M), p. 276.
19. RB (E), p. 131.
20. *Ibid.*, p. 110.
21. S-AF, p. 167.
22. RB (M), p. 242.
23. RB (E), p. 37.
24. *Ibid.*, p. 68.
25. *Ibid.*, p. 91.
26. S-AF, pp. 134-35.
27. *Ibid.*, p. 296.
28. *Soliloquies in England*, p. 251. Also ". . . it is in terms of essences that any possible physics is condemned to describe nature; but the description becomes true in so far as these or equivalent essences are actually embodied in the field of action." RB (M), p. 275. He has already said that such comparison or recognition of identity is impossible.
29. S-AF, pp. 101-02.
30. Cf. RB (T), p. 536.
31. This elementary problem of semantics was considered centuries ago by Aristotle in his work *On Interpretation* (cc. 1-9), and by St. Thomas in his commentary on that work.
32. RB (S), p. 664. Also "The sense of a moving existence is there most intensely present. . . . Animal watchfulness . . . asserts existence most vehemently." S-AF, p. 190.
33. On the two states of being, physical and intentional, of objects known, cf. St. Thomas, *Summa Theol.*, Ia, q. 78, aa. 3-4.
34. *Op. cit.*, p. 704.
35. Santayana allows no possibility for such distinction, and even explicitly tells us we "dream awake" and are subject to "normal madness."
36. On this point, cf. John of St. Thomas, O.P., *Cursus Philosophicus*, P. IV, q. 6, a. 1, Marietti, Turin, 1936.
37. Cf. St. Thomas, *Summa Theol.*, Ia, q. 85, a. 2.
38. In fact, he does so contradict himself: "Repetition is impossible in the realm of essence . . ." RB (E), p. 35; ". . . no two essences are ever identical." S-AF, p. 71; ". . . the identity of an essence with itself is absolute and constitutional." RB (E). On the other hand: "When I call an essence identical, I imply that I have considered it twice. . . ." S-AF, p. 151.
39. Cf. St. Thomas, *Summa Theol.*, Ia, q. 85, a. 5.
40. Cf. St. Thomas, *De Verit.*, q. 1, a. 3; *Summa Theol.*, Ia, q. 16, a. 2.
41. "Intuition though it always has a natural ground never can have a natural object, but only an ideal one. Nature has learned to

know itself at this price, that its knowledge should be indirect and symbolic." RB (S), p. 649. "What is there wrong or paradoxical in the fact that the sensations and reactions of an animal must express directly his own nature, and only indirectly the nature of the forces affecting him?" RB (T), p. 458.

42. For examples, cf. RB (S), pp. 556-57; S-AF, pp. 190-91; RB (S), p. 816; S-AF, p. 185.

43. "A General Confession," in *The Philosophy of Santayana*, p. 15.

44. *Soliloquies in England*, p. 257. Also "It is not the resemblance but relevance or closeness of adaptation that renders a language expressive or an expression true." S-AF, p. 88. "And if by the word truth we designate not the actual order of facts, nor the exact description of them, but some inner symbol of reconciliation with reality on our part, bringing us comfort, safety, and assurance, then truth also will lie in compromise: truth will be partly truth to oneself, partly workable convention and plausibility." *Soliloquies in England*, p. 83.

45. "Thus at last Mr. Santayana does not escape the legacy left by Locke: the spectrum of sense and the categories of thought are not imposed upon man by the world, but are original creations of the psyche." John H. Randall, "The Latent Idealism of a Realist," *Journal of Philosophy*, 28:24, Nov. 19, 1931, p. 655.

46. Cf. William Montague, *op. cit.*, p. 445.

47. B. H. Bode, "Critical Realism," in *Journal of Philosophy*, 19:3, Feb. 2, 1922, p. 77.

48. J. Arthur Ryan, C.SS.R., *Two Essays on American Critical Realism*, an excerpt from the dissertation *De Conceptu Dati in Realismo Critico Americano*, submitted to the Angelicum, Rome, 1935; reprinted from the *Revue de l'Université d'Ottawa*, vol. VI, April-June and October-December, 1936.

49. S-AF, p. 52.

50. *Ibid.*, p. 171. For statements expressing his own preference for illusions over realities, cf. RB- (E), p. 177; *ibid.*, p. 180.

51. *Soliloquies in England*, p. 252.

Epilogue

1. "A General Confession," in *The Philosophy of Santayana*, p. 8.
2. *Poems*, Constable & Co., Ltd., London, 1922.
3. *My Host the World*, p. 3.
4. *Ibid.*, pp. 139-43.
5. *The Idea of Christ in the Gospels*, pp. 89-90.

Bibliography

BY GEORGE SANTAYANA

Books

The Sense of Beauty, Charles Scribner's Sons, New York, 1896
Lucifer, A Theological Tragedy, H. S. Stone & Co., Chicago, 1899
Interpretations of Poetry and Religion, Charles Scribner's Sons, New York, 1900
The Life of Reason, Charles Scribner's Sons, New York
    Vol. 1, Reason in Common Sense, 1905
    Vol. 2, Reason in Society, 1905
    Vol. 3, Reason in Religion, 1905
    Vol. 4, Reason in Art, 1905
    Vol. 5, Reason in Science, 1906
Three Philosophical Poets, Harvard University Press, Cambridge, 1910
Winds of Doctrine, J. M. Dent & Sons, Ltd., London, 1913
Character and Opinion in the United States, Constable & Co., Ltd., London, 1920
Poems, Constable & Co., Ltd., London, 1922
Soliloquies in England, Constable & Co., Ltd., London, 1922
Scepticism and Animal Faith, Constable & Co., Ltd., London, 1923
Platonism and the Spiritual Life, Charles Scribner's Sons, New York, 1927
Some Turns of Thought in Modern Philosophy, Cambridge University Press, London, 1930
The Genteel Tradition at Bay, Charles Scribner's Sons, New York, 1931
The Last Puritan, Constable & Co., Ltd., London, 1935
Egotism in German Philosophy, J. M. Dent & Sons, Ltd., London, 1940
Dialogues in Limbo, Charles Scribner's Sons, New York, 1941
Realms of Being, Charles Scribner's Sons, New York, 1942, a single volume edition containing:
    The Realm of Essence

The Realm of Matter
The Realm of Truth
The Realm of Spirit
Persons and Places, Constable & Co., Ltd., London, 1944
The Idea of Christ in the Gospels, Charles Scribner's Sons, New York, 1946
The Middle Span, Constable & Co., Ltd., London, 1947
Dominations and Powers, Charles Scribner's Sons, New York, 1951
My Host the World, Charles Scribner's Sons, New York, 1953

(These books by Santayana are listed in the editions used by the author, either because of Santayana's preference for these editions or because they were personal copies that included valuable autographed marginalia. The thirtieth volume attributed to Santayana, which is not listed, is the revised and abridged *Life of Reason,* actually a work of collaboration with his secretary, Mr. Daniel Cory, and published posthumously by Charles Scribner's Sons.)

Articles

"Literal and Symbolic Knowledge," *The Journal of Philosophy,* August 1, 1918
"Some Meanings of the Word *Is,*" *The Journal of Philosophy,* July 3, 1924

Contributions

In *The Philosophy of Santayana,* Paul A. Schilpp, Ed., vol. II, The Library of Living Philosophers, Northwestern University, Chicago, 1940. Contains "A General Confession" and "Apologia Pro Mente Sua," the latter a reply to his critics writing in this volume. This work also contains a complete bibliography of Santayana's writings to 1940.

In *Twentieth Century Philosophy,* Dagobert Runes, Ed., The Philosophical Library, New York, 1947. Contains an essay, "Transcendental Absolutism."

In *The Philosophy of Santayana,* Irwin Edman, Ed., Modern Library, Random House, New York, 1942. Contains an essay, "Ultimate Religion."

In *Essays in Critical Realism*, Macmillan Co., New York, 1920. Contains an essay, "Three Proofs for Realism."

LETTERS

Personal letters to which reference is made in this book are in the possession of the author. The letter quoted in the second chapter of Part Two is dated Feb. 26, 1952. The letter quoted in the Epilogue is dated July 20, 1952.

BY OTHER AUTHORS

BOOKS

Adams, George P., Ed., *Contemporary American Philosophy*, Macmillan Co., New York, 1930

Ames, Van Meter, *Proust and Santayana, The Aesthetic Way of Life*, Willett Clark & Co., New York, 1937

Aquinas, St. Thomas
Marietti, Rome
Summa Theologica, Leonine text, 1948-50
Summa Contra Gentiles, 1934
De Veritate (*Quaestiones Disputatae*, vol. I), 1949
Commentaria in Libros Metaphysicorum Aristotelis, 1950
Lethielleux, Paris
De Ente et Essentia (*Opuscula Omnia*, t. I), 1941

Aristotle, *Basic Works*, Richard McKeon, Ed., Random House, New York, 1941

Bochenski, I. M., O.P., *La Philosophie Contemporaine en Europe*, Vaudou, tr., Payot, Paris, 1951

Brennan, Robert, O.P., *Thomistic Psychology*, Macmillan Co., New York, 1941

Cajetan, Thomas de Vio, *Commentaria in Summam Theolgoiae S. Thomae Aquinatis*, ed. Leonina, t. V, Rome, 1882
Commentaria in De Ente et Essentia S. Thomae Aquinatis, Marietti, Turin, 1934

Copleston, Frederick, S. J., *A History of Philosophy*, Burns, Oates & Washbourne Ltd., London, 1946

Descartes, René, *A Discourse on Method*, Veitch, tr., E. P. Dutton & Co., New York, 1912

Durant, Will, *The Story of Philosophy*, Garden City Co., New York, 1943

Duron, Jacque, *La pensée de George Santayana*, Nizet, Paris, 1950

Edman, Irwin, Ed., *The Philosophy of Santayana*, Modern Library, Random House, New York, 1942

Ferm, Vergilius, Ed., *A History of Philosophical Systems*, The Philosophical Library, New York, 1950

Gilson, Etienne, *Being and Some Philosophers*, The Pontifical Institute of Mediaeval Studies, Toronto, 1949

Gredt, Joseph, O.S.B., *De Cognitione Sensuum Externorum*, Desclée, Rome, 1913

Hume, David, *A Treatise of Human Nature*, Philosophical Works, vol. I, Little, Brown, Co., Boston, 1854

James, William, *Pragmatism*, Longmans, Green & Co., New York, 1907

Joad, C. E. M., *Guide to Philosophy*, Gollancz Ltd., London, 1948

John of St. Thomas, O.P., *Cursus Philosophicus*, vol. III, Marietti, Turin, 1936

Kant, Immanuel, *Critique of Pure Reason*, Meiklejohn, Tr., E. P. Dutton & Co., New York, 1934

Kinney, Sr. M. Cyril Edwin, O.P., *A Critique of the Philosophy of George Santayana in the Light of Thomistic Principles*, The Catholic University of America Press, Washington, D. C., 1942

Maritain, Jacques, *A Preface to Metaphysics*, Sheed & Ward, New York, 1948

Montague, William P., Ed., *Contemporary American Philosophy*, Macmillan Co., New York, 1930

Neill, Thomas P., *Makers of the Modern Mind*, Bruce, Milwaukee, 1949

Nöel, L., *Le Realisme Immediat*, Louvain, 1938

Oldegeering, P. Norbertus, O.F.M., *Georgius Santayana et Problema Epistemologicum*, Antonianum, Rome, 1950

Plato, *The Dialogues of Plato*, Jowett, Tr., Random House, New York, 1937

Runes, Dagobert, *Twentieth Century Philosophy*, The Philosophical Library, New York, 1947

Schilpp, Paul A., Ed., *The Philosophy of Santayana*, vol. II, The Library of Living Philosophers, Northwestern University, Chicago, 1940
Smith, Vincent E., *Idea-Men of Today*, Bruce, Milwaukee, 1950
Sullivan, James B., *First Principles in Thought and Being*, The Catholic University of America Press, Washington, D. C., 1939
Tante, Dilly, Ed., *Living Authors*, H. W. Wilson Co., New York, 1931
Toccafondi, E. T., O.P., *La Ricerca Critica Della Realità*, A. Arnodo, Rome, 1941
Turner, William, *History of Philosophy*, Ginn & Co., Boston, 1929
Valery, Paul, *The Living Thought of Descartes*, Cassell & Co., Ltd., London, 1948
Whitehead, Alfred N., *Process and Reality*, Cambridge, New York, 1929

ARTICLES

Bode, B. H., "Critical Realism," *The Journal of Philosophy*, Feb. 2, 1922
Calkins, Mary, "On Certain Difficulties in the Modern Doctrine of Essence," *The Journal of Philosophy*, Dec. 23, 1926
Cory, Daniel, "Some Notes on the Deliberate Philosophy of Santayana," *The Journal of Philosophy*, March 2, 1950
Dunbar, Olivia H., "Some Critics of the English Mind," *The Yale Review*, Oct., 1923
Farrell, Paul, O.P., "Portals of Doubt," *The Thomist*, July, 1945
Randall, John H., "The Latent Idealism of a Realist," *The Journal of Philosophy*, Nov. 19, 1931
Ryan, J. Arthur, C.SS.R., "Two Essays on American Critical Realism." Reprinted in booklet form, without indication of publisher, from original publication in *Revue de l'Université d'Ottawa*, vol. VI, 1936
Sellars, Roy Wood, "What is the Correct Interpretation of Critical Realism?", *The Journal of Philosophy*, April 28, 1927
Ten Hoor, Marten, "Santayana's Theory of Knowledge," *The Journal of Philosophy*, April 12, 1923

Index

Absolute, 30, 37, 45, 121
Abstraction, 34, 37, 80, 82, 107, 111, 142, 145, 160, 162, 164 ff., 181, 183
Aesthetics, 23
Alexander, 43
Aquinas, 5, 39, 48, 133, 144, 145, 160, 171
Aristotle, 4, 8, 20, 36, 37, 39, 48, 80, 121, 125, 133, 141, 153, 161, 170
Arnold, 32
Art, 20, 32, 56
Augustine, 17

Bacon, 36
Being, 5, 75, 82, 84, 127, 140, 154, 158 ff., 164, 167, 170 ff.
Bergson, 37, 38, 47
Berkeley, 29, 35, 40, 42, 50, 103
Bowen, 19
Bowne, 43
Bradley, 42
Brentano, 42
Broad, 43

Caird, John and Edward, 42
Cajetan, 160, 172
Calkins, 43, 181
Categories, 8, 34, 59, 69, 148
Causality, 51, 95, 97 ff., 166
Certitude, 6, 57, 69, 118, 137, 140 ff., 149, 156, 157, 174, 191
Cognition, 4, 8, 45 ff., 81, 85, 92, 102 ff., 132, 136, 150 ff., 157, 174 ff.
Concept, 38, 60, 84, 168, 180

Consciousness, 4, 7, 8, 45, 47, 49, 51, 55, 64, 65, 75, 86, 99, 103, 108, 115, 142, 151 ff., 177, 179, 187, 192
Cory, 163, 170, 188
Creighton, 43
Critical neo-realism, 9, 40, 41 ff., 102, 131, 150, 174, 181, 185, 186
Deism, 12, 42
Democritus 32, 38, 138, 153, 161
Descartes, 4 ff., 32, 35, 37, 41, 50, 69, 138, 141 ff., 151, 154, 184
Dewey, 43
Dialectic, 9, 16, 29, 30, 38, 39, 41, 58, 59, 61, 71, 106, 112 ff.
Dogmatism, 6, 30, 89, 146, 157, 191
Drake, 49 ff., 74

Eclecticism, 7, 21, 28
Egotism, 7, 33, 97, 185, 194
Empiricism, 3, 5, 30, 45, 137
Enlightenment, 12
Epicureans, 31
Epiphenomenalism, 40
Epistemology (epistemological question), 40, 44, 49, 52, 59, 74, 102, 104, 127, 131, 132, 141, 181, 186
Essence, 9, 10, 34, 35, 37, 40, 44, 51, 52 ff.
Ethics, 32, 37
Evolution, 30, 41, 50, 98 ff., 186
Existence, 5, 8, 25, 47, 52, 59, 60, 65 ff., 82, 88 ff., 111, 117, 118, 120, 122, 142, 145, 146, 148, 151, 155 ff., 164 ff., 191, 194
Extension, 7

INDEX

INDEX

Nominalism, 30, 37, 111, 174
Non-being, 83, 162, 167
Nunn, 43

Ontologism, 109

Palmer, 19, 32
Parmenides, 67
Paulsen, 19, 32
Perception, 30, 47, 48, 67, 84, 86,
103, 115, 116, 149, 181
Perry, 44 ff.
Phenomenalism, 8, 47, 48, 50, 142
Pitken, 44, 46
Plato, 4, 20, 28, 29, 36, 37, 40, 80,
84, 125, 158, 161, 162, 164, 183
Plotinus, 125
Pluralism, 43, 44
Politics, 27, 36
Positivism, 41
Pragmatism, 3, 30, 43, 45, 48, 117,
185, 192
Pratt, 49 ff., 74
Psyche, 86, 99, 107, 110, 113, 115,
148, 163, 175, 176
Psychologism, 34
Psychology, 29, 37, 57, 59, 99, 104

Rationalism, 3, 41, 42, 137, 187
Reason, 6, 36, 37, 41, 55 ff., 61,
70, 138, 155, 167
Reid, 193
Religion, 10, 12 ff., 19, 23, 25, 26,
31, 32, 35, 37, 64, 126, 142, 163,
180, 189 ff.
Rogers, 49 ff., 74
Rousseau, 12
Royce, 19, 20, 29, 32, 33, 43, 44,
88, 137
Russell, 43

Scepticism, 4, 5, 17, 28, 35, 36, 50,
61 ff., 116, 127, 134, 137 ff., 156,
157, 159, 177, 191

Schelling, 41
Scholastic philosophy, 4, 5, 38, 39,
132, 171
Schopenhauer, 33, 41
Science, 6, 20, 31, 34, 41, 45, 56,
57, 140, 180, 185
Sellars, 49, 51, 52
Sensation, 42, 45, 56, 79, 81, 103,
110, 111, 114, 140, 153, 160, 166,
176, 182
Sensism, 41
Sentimentalism, 42
Socrates, 4, 37, 139
Solipsism, 33, 35, 64, 67, 88, 134,
146, 159, 191
Sophists, 4, 138
Soul, 7, 121, 139, 155, 161, 175
Spaulding, 44, 46
Spencer, 29, 30, 31
Spinoza, 25, 31, 32, 33, 36, 38, 40,
50, 126
Spirit, 24, 35, 37 ff., 42, 84, 90, 91,
95, 99, 106, 108, 110, 111, 115,
119 ff., 163, 164, 169, 175, 184,
192
Stirling, 42
Strong, 19, 20, 49, 51, 74
Subjectivism, 4 ff., 41, 45, 109, 149,
151, 154, 176, 191, 192, 193
Substance, 32, 89 ff., 105, 108, 123,
155, 159, 160, 170, 176, 181, 186
Syllogism, 4, 5, 39, 57, 172

Taine, 29, 32, 36
Teleology, 3, 96, 97, 166 ff., 173
Temperament, 3 ff., 39, 42, 138,
163, 186, 190
Thales, 32
Thomistic philosophy, 5, 38, 48,
131, 133
Transcendentalism (transcenden-
tal criticism), 8, 33, 34, 37, 41,

· 233 ·

INDEX